New Directions in Theology Today

VOLUME I
Introduction

New Directions in Theology Today

WILLIAM HORDERN, GENERAL EDITOR

NEW DIRECTIONS IN THEOLOGY TODAY

Volume I
Introduction

BY
WILLIAM HORDERN

Philadelphia
The Westminster Press

LIBRARY OF CONGRESS CATALOG CARD NO. 66–15544

1. Theology, Doctrinal – History – 20th century

Published by The Westminster Press ®
Philadelphia, Pennsylvania

PRINTED IN THE UNITED STATES OF AMERICA

TO DAVIS WILLIAM

Editor's Foreword

Theology always has existed in some tension with the church. But there is considerable evidence that today the gulf is wider than ever. To both pastors and laymen it often seems that contemporary theology is working in opposition to the concerns of the parish. They are disturbed to read in newspapers and popular journals about theologians who seem to have lightly cast aside the cornerstones of the faith and who argue that the parish is doomed. To the theologian the parish often appears to be a respectable club dedicated to erecting buildings, raising budgets, and avoiding controversial issues.

There is little active dialogue between the theologian and the church today. The fault for this lies with both parties, but the situation is becoming increasingly serious as the church moves into a new age. This series is dedicated to the task of bridging the present gulf.

One of the reasons for the gulf between theology and the church is that neither the busy pastor nor the concerned layman can keep up to date with an ever-expanding theological literature. Thus, the purpose of New Directions in Theology Today is to present concise summaries of the present scene in theology. The series is not for the lazy pastor, nor for the layman who is beginning his theological education. Rather, these volumes are especially prepared for the busy pastor who is concerned with keeping abreast of modern theology and for the layman who, having been initiated into theology, is reading for further study, particularly to find out what contemporary Christian thinkers are saying.

The series is not written with the assumption that only professional theologians have something to say, but is offered in the hope that it will stimulate pastors and laymen to enter into the theological dialogue, and with the conviction that a vital theology for our time must be the work of the church as a whole.

WILLIAM HORDERN

Contents

Preface

When we plan an automobile trip we usually begin with a map of the whole country, upon which we find marked the main highways. With this we outline the general form of our trip. But after we have made the general outline, we want maps of states and of cities so that we can plan the trip in more detail. As the introductory volume of the series, New Directions in Theology Today, this book is meant to serve somewhat like the map of the whole country. It attempts to summarize the main issues and developments on the theological scene in recent years. The other volumes will concentrate upon specific doctrines and give a more detailed picture of smaller areas.

There have been times in history when a book of this size could have summarized adequately all the major theological developments of the day. But this is not such a time. Theology is going through an almost unparalleled period of diversity and change. Theological experiments are being pushed in a host of directions. It is not yet possible to tell which of these are dead ends and which are significant breakthroughs. In my attempt to give a map of the whole theological scene I have found that it is impossible to do justice to all the contemporary concerns and directions.

When one is forced to omit certain developments, critics will disagree with what is omitted. One can only defend oneself with the plea that later books in the series will fill the gaps. I am most disturbed by my failure to include the growing ecumenical dialogue between Protestant theology and Roman Catholic theology. But two things can be said about this omission. First, either the writer would have to spend considerable space on this development or else he would have to treat it only in passing, as I have done. Secondly, this development is so new that it has not yet made a significant impact upon Protestant theology as a whole. Thus it can be better treated within the context of particular doctrines where it has made its contributions.

As always with a book, many persons have contributed to the final form of this volume. Portions of it were presented to my classes at Garrett Theological Seminary, where student criticism was most helpful. I am indebted to Mr. and Mrs. Carl Geppert for graciously making their summer house available to me so that I could write free from distraction. I am grateful for Mrs. Richard Chaussee's work in typing the manuscript. Last, but not least, I am grateful to my wife for her usual role as reader and critic of my manuscript.

W. H.

CHAPTER I

Theology in Transit

The twentieth century could go down in history as one of the most lively periods in theology. Pitched battles have been fought as opponents have read each other out of the church. Dominant theological schools have risen to power and fallen. Theology has been pronounced dead but has risen to new life, and now there are theologians who tell us that it is not theology but God who has died. At the present moment theology seems to be in transit, and it would be a foolish man who would try to forecast what its destination will be.

When this century opened, liberal theology was rapidly moving to the fore in sophisticated circles. Harnack's book *What Is Christianity?* became a record-setting best seller. In it the ideas that had been maturing through Schleiermacher, Ritschl, and others were presented forcefully in a form that the average man could grasp.

Liberal theology threw Christianity into a determined confrontation with the world. It joyfully accepted the science of its time, including the debated hypothesis of evolution. It was happy to use the methods of historical criticism in its study of the Bible and it embraced the reigning philosophy of idealism as a tool to defend the faith. Liberals spoke confidently of looking at all facts, no matter how unpleasant, and letting the chips fall where they may. Refusing to hide behind dogmatic or authoritarian bulwarks, they allowed their faith to be exposed to the "acids of modernity." They were confident that they could change the traditional "categories" of Christianity without losing its "abiding truths." In men like Walter Rauschenbusch, liberal theology's social gospel launched an attack upon the evils of modern society.

Liberalism was obviously a theological position, yet it tended to disparage theology. When it took as one of its slogans, "The religion of Jesus, not the theology of Paul," it implied that true religion needs protection from theology. Theological subtleties, liberals charged, divide Christians from one another, discourage ethical endeavor, and lead to the identification of faith with the acceptance of "correct" doctrine.

Many liberals hoped to see the philosophy of religion replace theology. For example, E. S. Brightman defined the philosophy of religion as the systematic study of the whole field of religion by the use of methods, criteria, and authorities that are common to all philosophy. Brightman said that theology can take only two forms. The first, revealed theology, begins from a revelation that is put above reason. To Brightman such theology was an anachronism. The second form of theology, which he found among "most contemporary American Protestant thinkers," is simply a branch of the philosophy of religion. The only way in which it is distinguished from philosophy of religion is that instead of studying the whole field of religion, it restricts itself to one religion, such as Christianity. Even here, Brightman saw danger, because a preoccupation with one tradition "tends to produce a bias in favor of that tradition." For Brightman there was no future for theology separate from the philosophy of religion.[1]

As liberalism rose to the fore in Protestant circles, the defenders of a more traditional Christianity were thrown into confusion. By the second decade of this century many of them had gathered together in the fundamentalist movement. Although the fundamentalists could boast a number of first-class thinkers, the movement as a whole was soon maneuvered into a series of dead-end streets. Fundamentalists found themselves battling modern science and attacking the teaching of evolution in public schools. They split among themselves over issues, such as the timetable of the millennium, that did not seem important to most twentieth-century Christians. They split congregations and denominations. It sometimes seemed that fundamentalists were determined to prove that the liberal's fear of theology was justified.

While American Protestantism was being torn asunder by the liberal-fundamentalist controversy, theology was finding a new life in Europe. In 1919, Karl Barth published his commentary on Romans and started a new theological trend. Barth and his fellow "crisis theologians" rediscovered God's revelation as an answer to the sin of man. Biblical scholars, influenced by this theology, became less preoccupied with the "religion" of the Bible and with questions of who wrote what and when. Instead, they examined the "faith" of Israel and the early church and sought to develop a "Biblical theology."

As the currents of the new theology crossed the Atlantic, American theology was revitalized. Theological questions moved again to the center of interest in seminaries. A widespread theological interest arose among the laity and an extensive amount of literature was produced to interpret various aspects of theology for laymen. Courses in theology began to gain larger enrollments in colleges. In many cases clergymen found, to their embarrassment, that laymen were ahead of them in theological concern and sometimes in knowledge. The philosophy of religion, which had seemed destined to replace theology, now found that it was fighting for its life as it was attacked by the new theology and disowned by the philosophers.

As time passed, the new theology, now known widely as "neo-orthodoxy," began to show signs of diversity. We are beginning to realize that much confusion was created by the tendency to think of neo-orthodoxy as a third theological school, clearly distinguished from liberal and fundamentalist schools. In fact, such categorization gave a distorted picture of the situation. At times fundamentalism came close to a rather disciplined unity, but even at its high points, it contained significant diversity within itself. Liberalism was always a rather vague term that, in the United States at least, was used to denote anyone not obviously a fundamentalist. But the term "neo-orthodox" was the most misleading of all.

It is useful to speak of a "neo-orthodox movement" if we want to point up the fact that with the theological revival came a new appreciation of the traditional or "orthodox" forms of Christian faith. But since these were expressed in new and fresh forms, the newer theologies were never simply orthodox, they were *neo*-orthodox.

From the very beginning neo-orthodoxy bore within itself the seeds of radical diversity. So long as the new theologians concentrated upon a criticism of liberal and fundamentalist alternatives, a case could be made for calling them a school of thought. But as they expressed their positive ideas, it became apparent that neo-orthodoxy was a blanket term that had covered a number of different positions.

During the thirties the internal conflicts in neo-orthodoxy appeared as Barth and Brunner engaged in sharp debate. Bultmann and Gogarten moved in directions radically different from those of both Barth and Brunner. In the Scandinavian countries Nygren and Aulén had been rediscovering traditional Christian faith in a quite independent way. In Britain the Baillies and others who rediscovered traditional Christianity were inspired as much by the British tradition of men such as James Denney and P. T. Forsyth as they were by the continental theologians. In the United States the Niebuhrs and others produced a neo-orthodoxy that had more in common with the later Rauschenbusch than with Barth. When Tillich first came to the United States he was placed by Americans in the neo-orthodox camp, but as his thought became better known he was found to be radically different from both Barth and Reinhold Niebuhr.

The diversity within neo-orthodoxy became most evident during the forties when Bultmann regrouped European thought with his program of demythologizing. In the fifties demythologization began to stir America. At the same time the martyred German, Dietrich Bonhoeffer, inspired new theological trends.

As theology entered the sixties it became evident that it was in a state of flux. The old divisions into schools of thought had broken down, but the form of new schools had not yet taken shape. When one names the "leading theologians" in the sixties one is likely to use the same names that would have been used in the twenties and thirties, because no one else has arisen to take their place.

In part, the present situation in theology is the result of the upheavals and revolutions through which theology has passed during the last forty-five years. There is a need to take stock of where we have been before we can see clearly where we should go. It is not surprising, therefore, to find a motif of mediation and reconciliation in contemporary theology. Liberals are admitting that great truths are to be found in the "corrective words" of neo-orthodoxy. The neo-orthodox are now admitting that they were perhaps a bit hasty in casting out the insights of liberalism and so they are trying to pick up some of the pieces that were discarded in the heady days of early rebellion. The new conservatism that has arisen out of the older fundamentalism is irenic in spirit and is willing to appropriate insights from liberal and neo-orthodox positions even while it is determined not to capitulate to them.

The mood of mediation and reconciliation is most dramatic, however, in the ecumenical discussions of today. The gulf between Roman Catholic and Protestant may not have been bridged, but an active dialogue is going across it. The Protestant ecumenical movement has moved into something like maturity. It has not managed to produce an ecumenical theology as some hoped it would, but it has created an atmosphere in which persons of different backgrounds can meet and grow in mutual understanding.

At the same time that a mediating spirit is healing old theological wounds, new and more bitter battles are rising on other fronts. If one looks at the furor around the "Honest to God" debate, or the proposals for a secularized gospel and the "God is dead" theology, it is evident that new divisions have appeared. Even before the old wounds have been healed, new and perhaps deeper ones are being inflicted.

As the new debates take shape, it is evident that once again the very possibility of the theological enterprise is being questioned. The question has been raised on two fronts. Modern analytical philosophy has asked whether it is logically possible to speak of God. All statements about

God have been shown to be logically odd and perhaps logically impossible. Theologians were just beginning to meet this threat when another attack was launched from within theology itself. This attack has concentrated upon the sociological and psychological difficulties in speaking about God.

The sociological and psychological questions were first presented by Bultmann. He argued that modern man, living in a scientific age and presupposing a modern view of the world, could no longer think in terms of the Biblical "myths." When Bultmann first made his point in the forties he sounded dangerously radical to the guardians of traditional Christian faith. Today, however, Bultmann sounds strangely conservative. He still insists that we must speak of an act of God, but now there are theologians who tell us that psychologically our society is so conditioned that we cannot speak meaningfully of God. In this world that has "come of age," all talk about God is irrelevant to modern man. If the church is not to sink into oblivion in a "post-Christian" age, we are told, it must find ways of speaking that are "secular" and "worldly."

In the light of the various forces playing upon contemporary theology, its path into the future remains blurred. We have many voices proclaiming that they have the secret of what theology must do (or not do) if it is to speak to "modern man," but so far not one of these voices has been able to establish itself as dominant.

We could make a case that theology is moving in directions that are far more radical than was the earlier liberalism. Bultmann's program of demythologization goes beyond the position of most liberals. We hear an Anglican bishop calling the church to radically new expressions of faith and even suggesting that we may have to quit using

the word "God" for a generation. One young theologian
from Texas presents a Christian theology in which Christ
is not necessary to salvation and another young Texan develops a theology with Christ but without God. The day
of the radicals would appear to have dawned.

But before we can conclude that the radicals will carry
the day, we must note some other trends. The theology of
Karl Barth has just begun to make its real impact upon
America. Several books have appeared in recent years that
are interpreting Barth in a more favorable light than he
has hitherto enjoyed on this continent. Natural theology,
whose funeral was conducted without tears a few years
ago, is struggling to be reborn. Conservative theology,
rising out of the ashes of the old fundamentalism, is
speaking with a new force and with greater confidence
than it has for a century. Ecumenical discussion in general
and the conversation with Roman Catholicism in particular have inspired what we might call a Protestant "neo-
confessionalism" which has rediscovered power within the
traditional confessionalist positions of the various branches
of Protestantism.

The confused and transitional nature of contemporary
theology is evident when, turning from basic trends, we
look at particular Christian doctrines. For example, the
twentieth century has witnessed the theological rediscovery of the church. We have been reminded that the church
is not just another institution; it is itself an object of
faith. The liturgical revival continues to create appreciation for historic worship forms. And yet this is the day
when theologians declare that the church is so out of
date that it cannot continue to survive in its present form.
We hear that the church has become irrelevant because
it has lost touch with modern culture. At the same time

we hear that the church is sick because it has been cap-
tured by the modern culture. Contemporary theologians
can declare that today's theologian not only does not at-
tend church, he must be in radical opposition to the
church.

The relationship of theology to philosophy is another
point where the transitional nature of theology appears.
There are still theologians who declare that "Jerusalem"
has nothing to do with "Athens." But the real problems
arise when theologians decide to converse with Athens.
Where is Athens today? One wing of theology seeks a
correlation with existentialist philosophy. But what is
existentialism? Is Heidegger's system the existentialism
from which theology must learn? If so, do we turn to the
early or to the later Heidegger? There are theologians to
argue for both alternatives. Other theologians argue that
Heidegger is not a true existentialist, so they turn to Jaspers or Sartre or Camus. Still others cry, "A plague on all
your houses" and return to the pure fountainhead of
existentialism—Kierkegaard himself. Many theologians
argue that existentialism is not a living philosophy in the
Anglo-Saxon countries and that any attempt to draw on
existentialism will alienate theology even further from its
culture. Some of these have called us to learn from the
Anglo-Saxon analytical philosophers. Other theologians
have been busy recently trying to breath new life into the
philosophy of Whitehead. No longer can we ask with Ter-
tullian, "What has Jerusalem to do with Athens?"; today
we must ask what Jerusalem has to do with Athens, the
Black Forest, The Left Bank, Oxford, Cambridge, and
the University of Chicago. When both theology and philosophy are in chaos and transition, it is difficult to find
where they can speak to each other.

As one examines these paradoxical directions and themes of modern theology, it begins to look as though modern theology has mounted its horse to ride off in all directions at once. Where will this transitional stage of theology lead? Who will be the new Barths, Bultmanns, Tillichs, and Niebuhrs? Will theological revival and enthusiasm continue, or will we finally come to the eclipse of theology that has so often been foretold? This book does not pretend to answer such questions, but it does try to point out some of the chief landmarks so that the reader can find his way through the maze of contemporary theology.

CHAPTER II

The Demythologization Debate

The New Testament scholar Rudolf Bultmann raised a storm during the Second World War when he published a major article, "New Testament and Mythology."[1] The ensuing debate rearranged the schools of European theology. Since the late fifties this same debate has been an important factor in America.

Karl Barth pointed to a major irony when he said of Bultmann, "I know of no contemporary theologian who has so much to say about understanding, or one who has so much cause to complain of being misunderstood."[2] This is not simply the case of a thinker who has suffered distortion at the hands of his opponents, although that has happened. But even Bultmann's most ardent disciples charge one another with failure to grasp his thought, and those who are honestly concerned to understand him are often baffled.

There are probably several reasons for this confusion. For one thing, Bultmann often seems to have stated his position in a fashion that is vague or misleading. Secondly, it would seem that Bultmann has changed his mind at certain points without clearly saying so. Thirdly, confusion arises from his unfortunate choice of the term

"demythologization." (The German original, *Entmytho-
logisierung,* is no better.) A program of "demything" the
New Testament sounds rather like a soldier who is "de-
lousing" his bunk. The reader is prepared to see Bultmann leafing through the New Testament with scissors in
hand to eradicate the offensive sections. As we shall see,
this is not a helpful picture of Bultmann's intentions.
Finally, Bultmann makes considerable use of the early
philosophy of Heidegger. Inasmuch as Heidegger's thought
has baffled expert philosophers, it is not surprising that
Bultmann's use of Heidegger has created further problems
of interpretation.

It is not our concern to summarize Bultmann's controversial essay, since it is widely known. Neither is it our
concern to give a detailed analysis of Bultmann's position,
inasmuch as there are several excellent books that have
already done this. Our concern is to summarize the debate that Bultmann has aroused. We shall begin by ab-
stracting from Bultmann's essay eight theses that have
stirred up opposition and further development.

First, Bultmann affirms that the New Testament message comes to us within an ancient mythological framework. As examples of such mythology he cites the belief
in a three-storied universe that pictures heaven above and
hell below the earth, the supernatural intervention in this
world of either God or Satan, demon possession and divine guidance of human life, atonement through the
vicarious effects of Christ's death, the pre-existence of
Christ, the virgin birth, and the resurrection of Jesus.

The second thesis is that this mythology is incredible
to modern man with his world view. Since a man cannot
choose his world view at will, Christianity must be rejected by modern man if it insists upon belief in myth-

ology. One of Bultmann's chief concerns, therefore, is to show that Christianity does not depend upon primitive mythology.

The third thesis is that the real purpose of New Testament myth is not to give an objective picture of the world but to express man's self-understanding. Myth is not to be interpreted as a picture of the cosmos but as a means by which the writers understand themselves. As a result, we must not ask whether the myth correctly describes the universe but whether it is a true understanding of human existence.

The fourth thesis is that the New Testament itself demands demythologizing because its mythical positions are often contradictory. For example, sometimes it speaks of human life as being determined by cosmic forces and sometimes it calls men to make a decision. This implies that man is free. To overcome such contradictions, Bultmann believes that demythologization appears in the New Testament itself.

The fifth thesis is that we cannot simply eliminate myth. Bultmann believes that the great error of liberal theology was that it attempted to do this but in the process also eliminated the "kerygma," the essential message of the gospel itself. Thus Bultmann declares that theology's task is not to discard myth, as the term "demythologization" would seem to imply, but to interpret the myth existentially.

The sixth thesis is that the New Testament teaches that man loses his true life when he comes to depend upon the tangible material world, because his authentic life must be based upon intangible realities. To achieve authentic life, man must abandon all tangible forms of security and live in detachment from the world. Bultmann is careful to insist that this is not a call to asceticism. It is a way of life that lives in the world "as if" it did not. Although the authentic man uses the material world, he does not allow it to determine his life or become an ultimate concern to him.

The seventh thesis is that existentialist philosophy (i.e., Heidegger) has developed through philosophy alone, the same interpretation of human existence as the New Testament. The philosopher, however, makes the mistake of supposing that because man can see what authentic life would be, man can achieve this life by his own decision. The New Testament, however, knows that man's sinful state is such that man cannot, by his own efforts, achieve authentic life.

Here Bultmann makes a crucial distinction between "existential" and *"existentiell."* Philosophy can demonstrate that authentic life is an "existential" possibility for men. Human nature can be shown to be open to authentic life. But such a philosophical demonstration about human possibilities remains purely theoretical; it cannot give to a particular individual the power to make the necessary choices to achieve authentic life. That is, philosophy cannot create an *"existentiell"* possibility for a concrete individual. Here God's act in Christ is necessary. Before any individual can live an authentic life, he must be freed from his past. The forgiveness of God that comes through Christ gives to man this freedom. Furthermore, to live authentically is to love others, but before a man can love, he must first be loved. God's act in Christ reveals to each man that he is loved by God and thus gives him the *existentiell* freedom to love.

The eighth thesis is that Christian faith arises from the preaching of the Word and not from historical criticism.

OK. in sense of unpacking dialectical symbols.

To make his point, Bultmann uses two German words for history. *Historie* is the series of events that scientific historians, working impartially and objectively, are able to reconstruct as "what happened." *Geschichte,* however, is the past as it lives for a person today as he enters into it with decision and sympathy or antipathy. When an Englishman and an American stand at Valley Forge they may agree on the *Historie* of what happened there, but the *Geschichte* of Valley Forge will not be the same for both. For Bultmann the truth of Christian faith does not depend upon what *Historie* can verify; it is a matter of a man's personal response to the church's preaching of Christ. Thus, there is some truth in the claim that Bultmann has made his life's work as a Biblical scholar irrelevant to his theological position.

Each of the foregoing theses has raised controversy, but the demythologizing debate has revolved around three main issues. First, there was the question of what is meant by myth and whether the Christian can claim that the events of redemption are in any sense factual or objective. Secondly, there was the question of the legitimacy of Heidegger's philosophy as a framework for the exegesis of the New Testament. Finally, demythologizing raised the whole question of the relationship of history to the Christian faith. We shall look at the first two of these issues in this chapter and at the third issue in the next chapter.

FACT AND MYTH IN THE NEW TESTAMENT

Bultmann's program of demythologization first raised a controversy over the nature of myth and the factual basis for the New Testament's proclamation. In a real sense, this was a case of theology taking up unfinished business.

With the rise of Biblical criticism, theology had to ask how much of the New Testament narrative we could deny without losing the Christian faith. The fundamentalist-liberal controversy of the twenties centered on this. Fundamentalists argued that if we gave up belief in the objectively factual nature of Jesus' virgin birth and bodily resurrection or the New Testament miracles, we would lose the heart of the Christian faith. They insisted upon the verbal inerrancy of Scripture because this doctrine preserved for them the factual nature of such Biblical events. On the other hand, liberals denied that Christian faith depended upon belief in these events and were inclined to question the factual nature of some or all of them.

The fundamentalist-liberal controversy was not so much resolved as transcended. The various forms of neo-orthodoxy shifted the area of concern. God, the neo-orthodox affirmed, did not reveal doctrines or dictate words to men. He revealed his self, his nature, and his purpose through his "mighty acts" in history. The Word of God is not to be identified with the words of Scripture. God made himself known to the writers of Scripture, and as we read the Scriptures in faith, God will make himself known to us. The Bible is not an inerrant book of propositions to be believed, but a record of events through which God reveals his true self and through which he may enter into personal relationships with men. Because this approach centered on the Word that God speaks through the Scriptures, there was room for disagreement and agnosticism about the factuality of many of the events recorded. Thus Barth and Brunner could disagree about the virgin birth of Christ without it ever becoming one of their major disputes.

Bultmann's program of demythologization forced Christians to face again the question of the objective basis for many New Testament passages. The reader's first reaction to "New Testament and Mythology" is usually to assume that Bultmann denies the basic facts of New Testament history. A college student who read the essay during Holy Week was typical when he said, "Bultmann ruined Easter for me this year." Is this reaction justified? H. W. Bartsch is an editor of several volumes on demythologizing and something of an official interpreter of Bultmann. He argues that a misunderstanding developed when some of Bultmann's "ill-advised" disciples taught that Jesus did not perform miracles or rise from the dead. This, Bartsch claims, is not what Bultmann himself has said.[3] On the other hand, in answer to the philosopher Karl Jaspers, Bultmann says, "He is as convinced as I am that a corpse cannot come back to life or rise from the grave."[4] It is not surprising that such statements have led readers to assume that Bultmann denies that the resurrection did happen.

A major problem of interpreting Bultmann arises because the word "myth" does not have any one clear meaning. It is used in anthropology, psychology, literature, history, and philosophy as well as in theology, and its meaning varies with its context and use. It does not help discussion to ask if Bultmann is using the term "correctly," since there is no consensus as to its correct use. But it is helpful to ask if Bultmann uses his own definition of myth in a consistent fashion. In his original essay Bultmann defined myth as "the use of imagery to express the other worldly in terms of this world and the divine in terms of human life, the other side in terms of this side."[5] To illustrate, Bultmann refers to the use of spatial imagery to express divine transcendence, as when we say that

God is "high and lifted up." As such, myth necessitates its own criticism because it wants to speak of a transcendent power that controls man and the world, but its language is drawn from this world and thus obscures the very transcendence that it wishes to express.

After Bultmann's use of myth had been subjected to considerable criticism, he gave a further definition. Mythological thought, he affirmed, looks upon divine activity, in nature or in history, "as an interference with the course of nature, history, or the life of the soul, a tearing of it asunder—a miracle, in fact. Thus it objectifies the divine activity and projects it on to the plane of worldly happenings."[6] In the light of this further definition, Bultmann argues that myth is misleading because miracles or acts of God are never visible worldly events. They occur *in* worldly events, but they occur in such a way that they are hidden to all except the eyes of faith.

Bultmann seems to intend this second definition of myth to be simply an explication of his first definition, but on close examination, it would appear to be significantly different. If, with his first definition, we define myth as any use of imagery to express the otherworldly in terms of this world, then it would seem that any language about God must be mythical by definition. Man has no language except that which is drawn from his experience in this world. If he wishes to speak of the Christian God who transcends this world, he must use his worldly language. Thus Bultmann found himself forced to speak "mythologically," for he insisted that we must speak of an "act of God" in Christ. But, as the critics were quick to point out, an "act" is a term of this world and when "God" is made the subject of the verb "act," we are using the imagery of this world to speak of the other world. It seems that Bultmann's second definition of myth is an attempt to revise his first definition so that he can speak of God's "act" without becoming "mythical."

A debate continues among Bultmann's interpreters as to whether he uses the term "myth" consistently or not. Some argue that he does, more argue that he does not. To some critics it seems that Bultmann uses the term "myth" as a convenient means of discarding any concepts with which he disagrees.[7] Here we do not need to decide who is correct, although we might suggest that Bultmann's use of "myth" does not seem the best way for him to make his point.

As we study Bultmann in response to his critics it becomes evident that he is primarily concerned to see how we can speak about God. He emphasizes that we cannot speak about God on the basis of "objective" demonstrations of God's existence or activities. In part this is rooted in his philosophical view that authentic life is one that is based on "intangible realities." Thus the man who tries to base his faith on objectifiably verifiable events is living inauthentically. But Bultmann is also concerned to show that we cannot speak or think of God as another thing in the world of things, not even if we make God the greatest and best of the things.

The propositions of faith cannot be known in the way that we know statements about the physical universe, argues Bultmann. Faith propositions can be known only existentially, for to speak of God is always to speak of our own existence. To speak of God creating is not to refer to an objective event in the past that explains the origin of the universe, it is to confess that God is the Lord under whom the speaker is living.

Bultmann argues that his program of demythologization aims to extend the Paulinian and Lutheran doctrine of justification by faith alone into the realm of epistemology.

The man who believes in God must realize that he has nothing in his hand to bring. "He is suspended in mid-air, and cannot demand a proof of the Word which addresses him."[8] In the encounter of faith we depend upon God's ability to make himself known and not upon our ability to demonstrate or prove him, just as we depend upon his grace and not upon our works to save us.

When myth is defined as that which "objectifies" God's act or revelation, a confusion arises over the use of the word "objectify." In the first place, "objective" may be used to describe an observer who does not allow himself to become personally involved in that which he observes. When two persons quarrel, they may ask some disinterested person to give an "objective" view of the issues. Secondly, the word "object" is used to distinguish an inanimate thing from a person. Thus if we speak "objectively" about persons or about God, it may mean that we are speaking of them as though they were things. Thirdly, the term "objective" is used to denote that which exists apart from an observer or thinker. Thus I may say that the desk that I see before me is objective but that the red that I see when I press my eyeballs is subjective.

At least some of the dispute over demythologization seems to have arisen because the debaters have in mind different meanings of "objective." Bultmann seems primarily to be emphasizing that we cannot speak of God apart from our personal involvement. If it is really God about whom we are speaking, we must at the very moment of speaking be confessing our personal involvement with God. We must be speaking out of our relationship to God. Bultmann likens this to love about which a man cannot truly speak except when he speaks out of a loving relationship. Bultmann is also concerned to emphasize that we cannot speak of God as we can speak of the "objects" that we find in our environment. The critics, however, have feared that Bultmann's methods would lead to a denial of objectivity to God and his acts in the third meaning of the term. In this case, to speak of God would become just another way of speaking about certain aspects of the speaker's life and experience. They would not refer to any reality apart from the speaker.

As Gogarten explains it, the method of demythologization is a radical attempt to free history and theology from the pattern of subject-object thinking.[9] This pattern of thinking, rooted in Descartes and predominant in the natural sciences, distinguishes between the knowing subject and an object that is outside of him to be known. The problem of knowledge is thus to see the external object with as little "subjective" distortion as possible. But when we turn to history we find that we can no longer speak in this way, for history is not an object outside of the historian. The historian is himself in history; he is a part of what he studies. Similarly, we cannot speak of God as an object neatly separated from the speaker. He who would speak of God must speak of his relationship to God.

The kind of objectification that Bultmann rejects is one that would attempt to prove the content of faith apart from the decision of the hearers. When Bultmann argues that theology must be anthropology he means that to speak of God, the speaker must become involved and interested and must see that his own being is challenged to decision. There is no remote ground from which an onlooker may speak of God. Thus Bultmann continually repudiates all attempts to find a "secular proof" of the gospel. By a secular proof he means one that would be valid for any man regardless of his faith commitment.

There seem to be few of Bultmann's critics who would want to argue for "secular proofs" or to "objectify" our knowledge of God in the sense in which Bultmann wishes to deny it. The fear of the critics is that demythologizing will lead to a denial of any reality to God apart from man. As Gollwitzer sums it up: "Those who say 'encounter' must not shrink from also saying 'object', and thus from speaking of an objectivity of God; nor must they seek to banish the subject-object pattern from theology lock, stock and barrel, but must carefully state the sense in which they wish to transcend it and the sense in which it remains."[10] Gollwitzer clarifies his point by discussing the work of Herbert Braun and others, in which all objectivity is denied to God. "God" becomes simply a term to describe certain experiences of man. "With the introduction of the term 'God' there is of course nothing new added in the way of knowledge; it is only an 'expression' for a phenomenon which can also be expressed without it."[11] In such a case, the denial of objectivity to God results in atheism, the denial of all reality to God.

Bultmann certainly does not intend to advocate an atheistic denial of the "objectivity" of God. When Bornkamm suggests that for Bultmann the truth of the gospel is made to depend upon the hearers' decision when the Word is preached, Bultmann answers that this is a misunderstanding. "The meaning of the Christ event, as a thing of the past, doesn't depend on my decision. My decision means that I hear and open myself to the claim which is latent in this event."[12] Such a statement makes Bultmann's intentions clear. But the critics still ask whether, in fact, Bultmann's method can achieve the purpose he intends.

Ernst Kinder charges that Bultmann's fear of a secular proof results in making faith "a plunge into the totally uncertain darkness."[13] Bultmann, he argues, makes "theologically superior" anything that is uncertain.

Bultmann argues that we cannot ask for a criterion of revelation before the revelation itself appears, "as though God had to justify himself to man!" But philosopher Jaspers responds that it is not God who is being tested but the man who claims to speak in his name.[14] What reason, Jaspers asks, is to be given for listening to the preaching of the gospel rather than to the preaching of something else, such as Marxism. If a person claims to be speaking the truth, must he not point to something to justify his claim? If not, does he not end up pointing to himself?

Bultmann and his followers often argue that demythologization frees man from the "law" so that he can live by faith alone. Where others try to save themselves by vindicating their faith through a "secular proof," demythologization claims to free faith so that it can stand on its own feet. But that argument can cut both ways. To the critics it appears that demythologization is a new form of salvation by works. The act of faith, performed in the absence of objective evidence, becomes the work by which a man must save himself. Bultmann says that he applies to epistemology the theme, "Nothing in my hand I bring," but the critics charge that he would force God to remain empty-handed.

Since Bultmann and his followers have claimed to be simply followers of Luther, it may clarify the issues to look at Luther. We cannot expect that, in his time and place, Luther would have discussed the problem of the objective reality of the New Testament narratives. But Luther did face the Anabaptists, who argued that man can be saved by faith alone without dependence on such "objective" things as baptism. In his *Large Catechism*, Luther answered them by affirming that while nothing *in us* brings salvation except faith, "these leaders of the blind are unwilling to see that faith must have something to believe—something to which it may cling and upon which it may stand."[15] In other words, as Luther goes on to affirm, saving faith needs something external to which it can respond. We cannot be saved by our own works, but "God's works . . . are salutary and necessary for salvation."[16]

Luther's position seems clear. To save oneself by works means to perform some act by which salvation is secured, even if that act may be called "faith." The only defense against such "works righteousness" is to look to the events through which God acts and where one finds an objective basis for faith. Luther certainly would not present these events as "secular proofs," but neither does he envision a Christian faith that can ignore such an objective basis.

It is not surprising that the discussion of myth and objectivity has come to center on the stories of the resurrection of Jesus. From the point of view of Christian faith, the resurrection is not just another miracle; it is the very center of the faith. As Karl Barth says, "To put it sharply, while we could imagine a New Testament containing only the history of Easter and its message, we could not possibly imagine a New Testament without it."[17] Critics are fearful that Bultmann has eliminated the resurrection from Christian faith.

Bultmann argues that the cross and resurrection are not two separate events.[18] Upon this basis he can say, *"Faith in the resurrection is really the same thing as faith in the saving efficacy of the cross."*[19] He states unequivocally that "the resurrection itself is not an event of past history."[20] Such statements have led many critics to charge that Bultmann has abandoned the resurrection.

The question of the status of the resurrection in Bultmann is pointed up when he says: "But I cannot accept I Cor. 15:3-8 as kerygma. I call that line of argument fatal because it tries to adduce a proof for the kerygma."[21] The passage referred to by Bultmann is one in which Paul lists a number of those who witnessed the resurrection of Christ. It is dubious, however, that Paul intends this as a "proof" for his gospel. If we look at the passage in context, we find that Paul is not trying to prove Christianity to unbelievers; he is writing to a group who claim to be Christian. Since they have denied the resurrection of the dead, he writes to remind them of *what* was the gospel "which you received, in which you stand, by which you are saved." (I Cor. 15:1-2). Paul's purpose in this passage is to reveal a self-contradiction in the position of his readers. They accept a gospel which proclaims that Christ rose from the dead and yet they deny the resurrection of the dead.

Bultmann wants to make an important point. Faith is never an abstract knowledge of an event in the distant past. This is why he says that to speak of an act of God it is necessary to speak "simultaneously of myself as the person who is existentially concerned."[22] He wishes to affirm that Christians participate in the death and resurrection of Christ.[23] This is an important point: Christians are too often tempted to suppose that all one needs to do to be a Christian is to hold correct opinions about what happened in the past. Bultmann is also quite correct in affirming that the resurrection is an article of faith and that you cannot prove one article of faith by another. That is, you cannot use the resurrection of Jesus to prove that Jesus was and is the Christ. Anyone in the modern world who has attempted to do so knows that it cannot be done. Perhaps some of Bultmann's critics are striving to find such

thus God isn't dependent upon my resp; but God for me is.

a secular proof of the gospel, but it would appear that in most cases their concern is like that of Paul in the Corinthian passage. They are not trying to prove the gospel, they are trying to say what it is. And they are convinced that it does not consist of saying that the resurrection of Jesus was simply the rise of faith in the cross.

Perhaps we could clarify the issues if we distinguish between a proof, secular or otherwise, and a basis for belief. Few would argue that we can produce a proof of the gospel that would persuade any man regardless of his personal concern and commitment. But surely the believer has a basis for his faith. He is not engaged in a leap of wishful thinking.

One of Bultmann's helpful illustrations is his comparison of our knowledge of God with the knowledge of love between persons. Such love, he argues, is an event that "cannot be apprehended as love by objective observation, but only by myself who am encountered by it."[24] Obviously this is true. If I ask a man why he believes that his wife loves him, he may recite several of her actions and habitual forms of behavior such as her care for his needs, her interest in his affairs, and her loving acts toward him. But these are not proofs to me and I can always interpret them as exhibiting something other than love. Perhaps she acts this way because she wants his money or because he fulfills her need for a "father image." In a similar way the man of faith finds that the reasons that he gives for his faith are never proofs to the man who stands outside of faith.

The concern of Bultmann's critics can be brought out, however, if we imagine the case of a man who insists that his wife loves him but who cannot give any objective basis for saying so. He admits that she shows no concern about his health or interest in his work; she is unfaithful to him and shows no signs of repentance for it. How does this differ from the former illustration? In neither case can the man prove his claim that his wife loves him. The "proof" can come only to the one who is in the loving relationship. But in the first case we can see what the man means when he says that his wife loves him. In the second case we are not sure that we know what the man means when he says that his wife loves him. We wonder if he knows how to use the word "love." We become suspicious that his statement is not intended to tell us anything about his wife; it is simply an expression of his own need to feel that he is loved. Love is not an object like a stick or a stone that can be examined from the outside. But it is still meaningful to ask if the man's statement about his wife is an objectively true description of the wife or if it is only a subjective expression of the man's own feelings.

Bultmann has performed a service for theology in demonstrating that faith in God is not like a biologist's knowledge of the carcass of a frog. It is more like the knowledge that we have of another person's love for us. As love is not known from the outside but in the actual relationship, so God is known in the relationship of faith. But the critics fear that the demythologizer is like the man who asserts that his wife loves him but who can point to no loving acts on her part. Bultmann says that we must speak of an act of God, but the critics fear that he will not allow God to do anything when he "acts." For such reasons many critics remain unpersuaded that Bultmann has achieved his own stated purpose of affirming the reality of God and his acts. The debate continues.

The discussion of the objectivity of the acts of God forces us again to the old question of miracles. Often the exponents of demythologization fall back on Bultmann's early statement that it is impossible for modern man to believe in the miracle stories of the Gospels. Modern man holds to a world view that sees a closed universe with no room for a miraculous interference with the laws of nature. As Bultmann put it, it is impossible for man to use electricity and modern medicine and still believe in the New Testament world of demons and spirits.

This argument has met with considerable criticism. It was not a theologian but the philosopher Karl Jaspers who criticized Bultmann by asserting that modern science does not present us with a "world view" precisely because science has delivered us from all world views. Many college students have been confused by hearing in their religion courses that modern science has proven that miracles are impossible and then hearing scientists in the same college affirm that modern science does not know any reason why every miracle story related in the Gospels should not have happened. But this kind of argument seems to miss the crucial point.

There probably can be no resolution of the question of miracle so long as we think of a miracle as an intervention that breaks into the deterministic causal nexus of the physical universe. When Bultmann speaks of myth as "an interference with the course of nature," he seems to be using this definition of miracle. On the other hand, when he speaks of a miracle or an act of God as occurring in worldly events and hidden to all eyes except those of faith, he seems to be pointing to a fruitful way of handling the question. Unfortunately he has not worked this out as fully as we might have hoped.

Modern Anglo-Saxon philosophy has made it clear that there are different legitimate ways of explaining an event.

Although science can give a scientific explanation of any event, there are always other ways in which it can be explained. Thus, if my arm rises, the movement can be explained fully in terms of the causal pattern of electrical activity in my brain and nervous system which makes the muscles of my arm to contract and move the arm. But that explanation would be quite irrelevant in most cases. Usually we would want an explanation something like, "My purpose in raising my arm was to illustrate a point." In a metaphysical mood we may wonder how a purpose can "break into" the deterministic causal structure, but our failure to answer such a question does not make illegitimate the explanation in terms of purpose.

In the same way, we ought to see that to call something a miracle is not to speak about it in terms of the causal structure at all. A miracle is not made miraculous because the laws of nature are broken. To say of an event that it is a miracle is to say that God's will and purpose is made manifest in this event. If a man should be seen walking on water, that would not be, as such, a miracle. The modern scientist would be likely to describe this as a highly improbable but not an impossible event. No doubt the causal basis for it would be explained in terms of modern atomic theory. To call the event a miracle is not to deny the scientist's causal explanation; it is to argue that God's purpose is expressing itself through the event as my purpose expresses itself through the movement of my arm. It is to interpret the event as an "act" of God.

If the question of miracle could be discussed within some such framework, perhaps Bultmann and his critics could come closer to an understanding. But a basic problem probably would still divide them. Even if they agreed that they were not debating the causal basis of "miracles," there is still the question of how the act of God is to be interpreted. Is Heidegger's philosophy a useful form of interpretation? Is the purpose of Scripture to give us self-understanding or is it to give us an understanding of God? Or is it both? In short, we come to the next issue of the demythologizing debate, the question of existential exegesis.

EXEGESIS AND EXISTENTIAL INTERPRETATION

The second basic question in the demythologizing debate raises the problem of how to interpret the New Testament. In technical language, it is the problem of hermeneutics. Does Heidegger's philosophy serve as an adequate tool for bringing the New Testament message to modern man?

Bultmann has been deeply concerned with the hermeneutical question. He is concerned with the problem of the man who must preach the gospel. How can we make the Bible, with its ancient world view, meaningful to twentieth-century man? Hermeneutics, says Bultmann, must go beyond a mere analysis of form and grammar; it must seek an understanding of the "life moment" of the writers. There can be no communication until the exegete finds a common ground of understanding with the author. As a result, the exegete must come to the text with a "prior understanding" of the subject in question.

A "prior understanding" sounds ominous. Is Bultmann justifying the exegete in making up his mind before he looks at the text? Many critics would say that this is what Bultmann does, but it is quite clear that this is not what he intends to do. His point is that to understand any text we must have some idea of what it is speaking about or we cannot comprehend it. For example, a text dealing with

N.B. To unpack d.s.'s must have experienced the event symbolized.

music can be understood only by someone who already knows something about music. Bultmann concludes, *"The presupposition for understanding is the interpreter's relationship in his life to the subject which is directly or indirectly expressed in the text."*[25] The exegete, from out of his life interests, will have his own questions which he must put to the text in question.

Whenever we read philosophy or religion, our primary concern is to raise questions about "human being" as "one's own being," states Bultmann. To ask the interpreter to silence his subjectivity and individuality in order to get an "objective" view of a philosophical or religious text is absurd. It would make it impossible to understand the kind of question with which such a text is wrestling. Of course, affirms Bultmann, we must not allow our prior understanding to dictate the results of exegesis, but without a prior understanding, rooted in our personal interest, there can be no exegesis.

At first sight it appears impossible to apply such an approach to the interpretation of the Bible. The Bible speaks of an act of God, but how can we know what an act of God is until we actually meet one? This is only an apparent contradiction, believes Bultmann. We cannot know how Socrates died unless we are told the story of his death. But if a man is to understand the story of Socrates' death, he must first know what it means for a man to die. In the same way, we cannot know before reading the Bible *what* God's act will be. Nonetheless, to understand what God's act will be, we must first know what an act of God is.

Before man reads the Bible, he can know what an act of God is, says Bultmann, because in man as man "an *existentiell* knowledge about God is alive in the form of the inquiry about 'happiness,' 'salvation,' the meaning of the world and of history, and in the inquiry into the real nature of each person's particular 'being.' "[26] Bultmann links his point to Augustine's famous statement that our hearts are restless until they find their rest in God. Man is seeking God and asking the questions to which God is the answer even though he may not be aware of it. This is the prior understanding which makes the Bible meaningful. This is why Bultmann insists that we cannot talk about God without also talking about man or, more concretely, talking about ourselves.

There is still an important problem for Bultmann. Gustav Brøndsted agrees that the gospel does presuppose a prior understanding but this "consists in *being* human, not in a philosophy about human existence."[27] If, he argues, we begin with a particular philosophy of human existence, such as Heidegger's, we are doomed to systematize our understanding of man so that we predetermine what the Scripture can say to us.

To defend his use of Heidegger, Bultmann distinguishes between a "scientific exegesis" and a "simple heed." Simple heed describes the man who goes to Scripture to let it speak to his life. Scientific exegesis, on the other hand, aims to interpret the Scripture for man in general by reflecting on the nature of human existence in general. Such reflection is the task of philosophy. Thus, to exegete the New Testament in terms of its meaning for human existence, we must look to the philosophy that has developed the concepts through which human existence can be discussed.[28]

Every reader of the New Testament, asserts Bultmann, will interpret it by raising, implicitly or explicitly, certain questions for it to answer. The man who turns his "simple heed" to the New Testament will have his preunderstanding, but it may be an unconscious one. This man must make his own decision about what the gospel means for his life. No philosophy can tell him what his encounter with the Word of God ought to be. His response, in traditional terminology, is "the work of the Holy Ghost."[29] On the other hand, scientific exegesis is trying to understand what the text means not "to me" in this moment but to men in general. Consequently it must use an understandable terminology drawn from some philosophy. It must, therefore, seek for the "right" philosophy, the one that most adequately describes what it means to be human.

In Bultmann's mind, Heidegger's philosophy is the "right" one. This does not mean that Bultmann slavishly follows Heidegger, nor that he rules out all help from other philosophers. He does believe that Heidegger's analysis of human nature is in harmony with the New Testament, so that it provides us with a useful language in which to express the Christian understanding for modern man.

The criticism of Bultmann's use of Heidegger's philosophy can be divided into three types. First, there are those who argue that Bultmann is guilty of philosophical inadequacies. Secondly, there are those who argue that the use of Heidegger leads Bultmann to theological distortion. Thirdly, there are critics who argue that the use of Heidegger defeats its purpose because it divorces us from the modern men to whom it is addressed. We shall make a brief summary of these critiques.

Because Bultmann rests so heavily on the work of Heidegger, one could expect that philosophers of other schools would not be too happy. Their complaint is registered forcibly by Karl Jaspers. He charges, "Because Bultmann confines philosophy to one book by Heidegger, and, as I suspect, misunderstands that book when he emphasizes its 'scientific,' objective, scholastic aspect, he in effect cuts himself off from all philosophy."[30] Jaspers says that Heidegger does not present *the* fundamental experience of human existence but *a* fundamental experience. Heidegger's philosophy contains, he believes, a fundamental ambiguity in that it uses existentialist terms but strives at the same time to operate scientifically and phenomenologically. If there is anything that is common to all philosophies called existentialist, it is their rejection of "so-called scientific philosophy," argues Jaspers.[31]

Jaspers seems to be saying that existentialism is a revolt against those philosophies which, as Kierkegaard put it, reduce the individual to "a paragraph within a system." This is rejected because a system is by definition coherent but an individual's life is paradoxical. A system can only be a matter of thought, but an individual's life must be lived. Because Kierkegaard believed that Christianity deals with life, not with systems, he was sure that anyone who read the New Testament in the light of a system would misread it. Jaspers' argument thus gives philosophical support to the theologians who argue that Bultmann's use of Heidegger has led to a distortion of the New Testament.

Bultmann believes that he has met this objection with his distinction between existential and *existentiell*. Heidegger, he affirms, only helps us to see the general existential possibilities for human nature. The individual reading the New Testament still has to make his individual *existentiell* decision. But critics fear that existential interpretation, when interpreted as the "correct" philosophy, provides a strait jacket that limits the *existentiell* possibilities for any individual as he reads his New Testament.

Theologian Heinrich Ott also makes a philosophical criticism. Ott points out that Heidegger has changed the direction of his thought from his earlier work, *Being and Time,* upon which Bultmann relies. In particular, he argues, Heidegger no longer sees his work as providing a "scientific" description of man. By building on the later Heidegger, Ott believes that he can work with a philosophy that does not provide a "preunderstanding" of man, and hence theology is free to think from the position of faith. In fact, Ott believes that the later Heidegger provides more support for Barth's theology than for Bultmann's thought.[32]

Jaspers and Ott represent the philosophical criticism of Bultmann that charges that he has put too much emphasis upon one philosophical book which he may have misunderstood. But there is another philosophical criticism which chides Bultmann for not going all the way with philosophy. This is represented by Fritz Buri and Schubert Ogden.

Basic to Bultmann's position is the affirmation that man, apart from revelation, can see what authentic life is. As a result, man can recognize the inauthentic nature of his life. When Heidegger describes the nature of authentic and inauthentic life, Bultmann believes that he is "saying the same thing as the New Testament and saying it quite independently."[33] This is why Bultmann believes that theology can use Heidegger's existential description of human nature. Bultmann breaks with Heidegger, however, because Heidegger believes that, having seen what authentic life is, a man can obtain it through his own efforts. Bultmann replies that this fails to recognize the full extent of man's sinful condition. The sinner may know what authentic life would be, but this knowledge does not give him the power to achieve such a life. The sinner can achieve authentic life only when he hears the gospel which tells him that God has acted for him in Christ. When he knows that he is loved and forgiven, he is freed to love and forgive others. To many critics it seems that Bultmann is inconsistent when he follows philosophy this far and refuses to go the rest of the way.

Fritz Buri is one of these critics. He charges that Bultmann quit his task of demythologization too soon. We must go beyond demythologizing the New Testament—we must also "dekerygmatize" it. That is, we must no longer speak of an act of God, nor of salvation through Christ. Instead, we need to see the New Testament as a profound analysis of the human condition and as a guide to help man achieve authentic life for himself.

Schubert Ogden makes a similar point in his criticism of Bultmann. Ogden affirms that Christ clarified what was, and is, always open to man. Hence man can achieve authentic life without Christ. He says, "Christian faith is to be interpreted exhaustively and without remainder as man's original possibility of authentic existence as this is clarified and conceptualized by an appropriate philosophical analysis."[34]

At first sight it would seem that Ogden has escaped the inconsistency that he finds in Bultmann's claim that philosophy can analyze the nature of authentic life but that only Christ can make it a possibility for a particular person. Ogden, however, falls into an inconsistency of his own. On the one hand he sees Christianity as a human possibility that can be analyzed "without remainder" by philosophy, but on the other hand he affirms that "the sole norm of every legitimate theological assertion is the revealed word of God declared in Jesus Christ, expressed in Holy Scripture. . . ."[35] If Bultmann was inconsistent when he broke with philosophy to affirm the necessity of Christ for man's salvation, as Ogden charges, is not Ogden equally inconsistent when he breaks with philosophy to affirm the necessity of Scriptural revelation for theology? Must not the philosopher consider that Ogden's norm is arbitrary? Is Ogden's theologian bound to a particular text, while the philosopher can gain the same truth by roaming freely through human experience?

Buri and Ogden agree that Bultmann falls into an inconsistency. Buri frees himself from the inconsistency by abandoning the Christian message itself. Ogden abandons much of the Christian message but is left with his own inconsistency. Is it possible to resolve Bultmann's inconsistency without dissolving the Christian faith?

The second group of Bultmann's critics attack the theology that results from his use of philosophy. They find that Bultmann's inconsistency arises from the error of supposing that existentialism, as found in the early Heidegger, is an adequate terminology to express the message of the New Testament. They charge that Bultmann's use of Heidegger has resulted in his coming to the New Testament with a "prior understanding" that causes him to distort its meaning.

Does Heidegger illuminate or distort New Testament themes? In his original essay on demythologizing, Bultmann summarizes Heidegger by saying:

For him the chief characteristic of man's Being in history is anxiety. Man exists in a permanent tension between the past and the future. At every moment he is confronted with an alternative. Either he must immerse himself in the concrete world of nature, and thus inevitably lose his individuality, or he must abandon all security and commit himself unreservedly to the future, and thus alone achieve his authentic Being.[36]

This passage is far from being crystal-clear, but most students of the New Testament are amazed to hear Bultmann ask of it, "Is not that exactly the New Testament understanding of human life?" In the New Testament, man is at times pictured as existing in tension, but never is the tension adequately described as being between simply the past and the future. New Testament man is faced with the tension between obedience and disobedience to God. He is faced with the tension of choosing which God he will serve and worship. He is faced with a tension between a future of sin and a future of grace. In the New Testament, man is called to commit himself unreservedly to Christ, not to the future.

Central to Bultmann's thesis is the assumption that Heidegger's concepts of inauthentic and authentic life correspond to the New Testament concepts of sin and the new life in Christ. But Heidegger clearly announces that he interprets man's existence without any reference to God. Can Heidegger be saying the same thing as the New Testament when the latter's view of sin and salvation always presupposes that man was created to be God's son?

This point is pressed home by Barth. He charges that Bultmann has fallen into the old pitfall of Protestant orthodoxy in assuming that we can define sin apart from God's act to save man. But in the New Testament, sin becomes understood only when it is revealed that man's true destiny is to live, not for the future, but for God as God's son. In short, the New Testament understanding of both sin and salvation depends upon the revelation of God in Christ which reveals to man a possibility that man neither knew nor had before it was revealed.

Helmut Thielicke goes farther. He charges that "what the philosophers regard as the authentic ego of man is, from the Christian point of view, still fallen man."[37] A close study of Heidegger shows that Thielicke's charge is not unfounded. Heidegger defines man's authentic life in terms of a man's loyalty to his own self.[38] Furthermore, he declares that the authentic man repudiates all standards apart from himself, whether those standards come from God or from his fellowmen.[39] As such the authentic life in Heidegger bears suspicious resemblance to the Reformer's picture of sinful man as "curved in on himself" or to Brunner's doctrine of sin in terms of "man in revolt."

In a carefully constructed critique, Gollwitzer points out that Bultmann's use of Heidegger means that Bultmann begins with the assumption that man is anxious because he knows about authentic life and fears that he has lost it. Such a man's concern with the New Testament is limited to what it can tell him about gaining what he already wants. Instead of listening to the concerns of the New Testament, man comes to the New Testament with a pragmatic concern that he hopes to have met. This means that "God can now only become perceptible in his function of serving men's interest in authenticity."[40]

Gollwitzer extends his argument to include the whole school of existentialist theologians. We have seen that Bultmann uses existentialist categories as a way of arriving at the "self-understanding" of the New Testament writers. New Testament myth is not meant to describe the universe but to illustrate the writer's self-understanding. Other theologians have carried this even farther than Bultmann. Gollwitzer finds that such an approach distorts the obvious meaning of the New Testament. It is true that the New Testament writers had a new understanding of themselves. But they had this because of the new light that came to them in Christ. They understood themselves differently because, in Christ, they had come to understand God differently. The most important thing to them was the revelation in Christ and their new vision of God. But, charges Gollwitzer, when we go to the New Testament wearing the spectacles of existentialist philosophy, we have to turn the New Testament upside down. What was

of first interest to its writers, the events in which God revealed himself in a new way, becomes of secondary importance and sometimes even irrelevant to the existentialist
exegete. On the other hand, that which was a secondary
consequence for the New Testament writers, their new
self-understanding, becomes of primary importance. We
are no longer interpreting what the New Testament says;
we are changing it into what it would have said if it had
been written by twentieth-century philosophers and not
by first-century Christians.

Other theologians have made similar arguments to show
that Bultmann's reliance on Heidegger has distorted other
features of the New Testament. For example, eschatology
in Bultmann loses its New Testament reference to a future
time and life and becomes simply a way of expressing the
possibility of authentic life here and now. To such critics
it seems that Bultmann's reliance upon Heidegger has
become a quicksand in which the New Testament has dis-
appeared from sight.

Bultmann draws upon Heidegger's philosophy because
he hopes that the use of this modern philosopher will help
to bring the modern world into conversation with the
New Testament. The first two groups of critics have aimed
their criticism at the way in which Bultmann uses Heidegger and have charged that he distorts either Heidegger or
the New Testament. But the third group of critics believes
that Bultmann's major error is in supposing that Heidegger speaks either for or to modern man.

Sometime ago Austin Farrer suggested that the modern
man to whom Heidegger could speak is about one out of
every five thousand living men.[41] Nonetheless, for a considerable period the demythologizing debate did not seriously question the premise that Heidegger did speak for
modern man. It is only recently that critics have arisen to

charge that Heidegger's way of thought is so totally alien to the modern world that any interpretation based on Heidegger is doomed to be irrelevant today.

Paul van Buren makes this objection when he wonders where the "left wing existentialist theologians" have found their "modern man."[42] Harvey Cox takes the argument farther. Existentialism, he says, arose as the response of the educated European middle class to its loss of power in the twentieth century. This class, which had run Europe in the eighteenth and nineteenth centuries, was pushed aside in this century by technicians, scientists, social planners, and political revolutionaries. Because its life had become meaningless, it created the existentialist philosophy, which interprets all life as meaningless.

Cox thus implies that when theology uses existentialism as its road to modern man, it is doomed to fail. Instead of speaking to modern man, it is dealing with a passing social class. Cox finds this illustrated when existentialist theologians translate the Biblical myths into "yesterday's metaphysics" in the vain hope that as such they will speak to modern man. To win modern man, the existentialist theologian finds himself in the awkward position of having "first to lure people into existential vertigo as a kind of preparation for preaching."[43]

Cox's attack upon existentialism loses some of its force because of his tendency to try to refute a philosophical position by an appeal to its social history. This is a logical fallacy of the first order. But van Buren and Cox do point up an undeniable fact: the American mind, at least, finds existentialist "preunderstanding" more difficult to grasp than the New Testament stories themselves. Insofar as demythologizing is an attempt to bring the gospel to modern man, Heidegger's existentialism is an unwieldy tool for its use.

It would appear that theology is moving beyond the demythologizing debate to other concerns. But the debate has left an indelible mark on twentieth-century thinking. The theological period of the thirties and forties was dominated by Barth. This does not mean that he persuaded the majority of theologians; it means that his questions had to be faced by all theologians. In a similar way Bultmann dominated the theology of the fifties. Today it is impossible to write theology as though demythologization had not appeared among us. Its legacy lives on.

Because of Bultmann, theology is keenly aware of the hermeneutical problem. How *can* we interpret or translate the Biblical message so that it comes home meaningfully to man today? We see that Bultmann was right when he said that modern man often does not reject the gospel: he cannot hear the gospel because he is alienated by the forms in which the gospel is spoken to him. This is not to assume that once modern man does understand the gospel he will accept it, but it does see the need for speaking so that modern man makes his decision about the gospel and not about the inadequate forms in which it is presented. Several of Bultmann's disciples are now at work in seeking to build a "new hermeneutic."[44]

Perhaps the most important legacy of demythologization is that it has forced theology to listen to the world in which it lives. Is it possible to find a philosophy or way of thinking in the modern world that can be a means through which the gospel can be spoken to modern man? As theologians have listened to their world, they have not always agreed with Bultmann about the nature of modern man. There appear to be few today who would accept Bultmann's analyses or programs. But Bultmann's questions still haunt us.

CHAPTER III

History and Kerygma

A third area of debate into which demythologization led was that which dealt with the relationship of history to Christian faith. Because this debate has moved farther from Bultmann than the others, we are treating it in a separate chapter. Furthermore, since another book in this series will deal with this problem we shall not attempt to give a full summary of it.[1] Our object is simply to see how this problem fits into the wider concerns of contemporary theology.

The question of history and faith is almost an inevitable one for Christianity because it is a historical faith. Whereas other religions have looked to nature and mystical or rational experience to find the revelation of God, the Biblical faith finds revelation primarily in certain historical events. Typically, we find that Biblical revelation includes two elements—a historical event and its interpretation by an inspired prophet or apostle.

As a classic illustration of the nature of Biblical revelation we may take the sixteenth chapter of Matthew. Jesus asks his disciples, "Who do men say that the Son of man is?" (Matt. 16:13), and they respond by telling various theories that are being advanced. Then Jesus asks, "But

who do you say that I am?" (Matt. 16:15), and Peter responds by saying, "You are the Christ, the Son of the
living God" (Matt. 16:16). Jesus commends Peter for these
words and says, "Flesh and blood has not revealed this to
you, but my Father who is in heaven" (Matt. 16:17).

This incident illustrates how God's revelation includes
a historical event, in this case the life of Jesus. But it is
not known as God's revelation until it is interpreted by
the inspired apostle. The event is open to other interpretations and thus it is a challenge for those who have eyes to
see and ears to hear.

This understanding of revelation involves Christian
faith in a complex relation to history. Because many who
saw Jesus as he lived in Palestine did not believe in him
as an act of God, we cannot suppose that a historical veri-
fication of the Gospel records would prove to all men that
he is. On the other hand, if historical study should demonstrate that Jesus never lived, it would destroy Christian
faith since Christian faith is not a collection of truths that
could be true apart from Jesus. As Bultmann says: "New
Testament faith is always *faith in Christ*. Faith, in the
strict sense of the word, was only there at a certain moment in history. It had to be *revealed*, it *came*."[2]

If an uninitiated layman or parish clergyman walked in
on a modern theological discussion, he might believe that
he had entered some "Alice in Wonderland" territory. He
would find theologians seriously asking if the "kerygmatic
Christ" (i.e., the Christ preached by the church) is the
same as the Jesus of history. He would hear some arguing
that Christian faith has no interest in the historical Jesus.
He would hear that faith can be neither helped nor hin-
dered by knowledge of the historical Jesus. This would
sound weird to the layman because, as J. Jeremias puts it:
"To anyone who is not aware of the controversy, the ques-

tion whether the historical Jesus and his message have any significance for the Christian faith must sound absurd. No one in the ancient church, no one in the church of the Reformation period and of the two succeeding centuries thought of asking such a question."[3] To understand the current situation in theology, we must recall some history.

During the nineteenth century a host of scholars pursued a search for the "historical Jesus." Behind this search lay certain basic presuppositions. First, it was taken for granted that the Gospel records of Jesus are, in large part, the product of the early church's imagination and theological speculation. Secondly, there was the conviction that the methods of historical criticism, as developed by secular historians, could locate the hard core of historical facts and thus present us with Jesus as he really lived. Thirdly, it was implied that this historical Jesus, when found, would be a hero of faith who would inspire modern man to live a more noble life.

The nineteenth-century search for the historical Jesus failed. Its failure became apparent when each historian produced a different version of Jesus. It was as though the historians were playing the television game and asking, "Will the real Jesus please stand up?" The problem was that a different Jesus stood up for each historian. Albert Schweitzer's monumental study, *The Quest of the Historical Jesus,* documented these differences. He said, "Thus each successive epoch of theology found its own thoughts in Jesus; that was, indeed, the only way in which it could make him live."[4] Ironically enough, Schweitzer illustrated his point when he went on to develop his picture of the real Jesus and likewise produced his "own thoughts." Instead of giving us the Jesus of history, the nineteenth-century quest gave us the Jesuses of the historians.

About the same time that Schweitzer was making his

historical critique of the nineteenth-century search, Martin Kähler was making a theological critique of it. Attempting to be "a protector of the simple Christian from the new papacy of the historian," he argued that the historical critics had played fast and loose with the Biblical material. They began by presupposing that Jesus was merely a man and thus anything that did not fit their nineteenth-century view of man was rejected as legend and myth. In other words, before even examining the Biblical records, these historians had decided that many portions of them were untrustworthy. But, argued Kähler, the only Jesus that we know is the Jesus whom the Biblical writers preached as the risen Christ who is the Lord. The writers were not concerned to give us the bare facts of history but to proclaim the one through whom they had found salvation.

It was Kähler who first made the distinction between *Historie* and *Geschichte* that Bultmann uses. To Kähler it was obvious that the Gospels must be read as *Geschichte* and not as *Historie*. That is, the Gospels are not dead records of the past. For both authors and readers they are living messages.

Kähler and Schweitzer discouraged the search for the historical Jesus, but it was the rise of form criticism that seemed to render its death blow. This method of historical study directed the scholars' attention to the "life situation" in which the Gospels were written. It found the Gospels to be proclamations of faith, dominated by the concern of the church at the time of writing, and not historical treatises. The hope of writing a biography of Jesus was largely abandoned.

Through a strange irony the work of Bultmann has inspired a new search for the historical Jesus. Bultmann certainly did not intend to do this. As a form critic, Bultmann went much farther than most scholars in denying the historical validity of the Gospel narratives. But he did not see this as a misfortune for Christian faith. For Christians, he affirmed, the Christ that matters is the Christ who lives in the words of the church's preaching. In the proclamation of the gospel we do not meet Jesus as a person of past history; we meet him as the "eschatological phenomenon" who forces us to a decision. All that we need to know about Jesus is that he came and died and is now proclaimed by the church as Lord and Savior. To ask for more historical knowledge of Jesus is to seek salvation by works.

A number of Bultmann's disciples began to fear that his position was leading to a new docetism. They argued that unless we can believe that the Christ proclaimed by the church is also the Jesus of history, we have a docetic Christ, a divine figure who lacks true humanity. These disciples feared that Bultmann was presenting a philosophy of human existence that was attached rather precariously to the empty historical fact that Jesus once lived.

The concern to escape docetism motivated a group of Bultmann's disciples to undertake what has become known as a "New Quest" for the historical Jesus. Men like Fuchs, Käsemann, Ebeling, and Bornkamm have attempted to show that enough can be rediscovered about the historical Jesus to indicate that there is a real continuity between him and the faith of the church about him. These men have been persuaded by Bultmann that history cannot prove the Christian faith. But they have argued that it could disprove the faith. As Ebeling puts it, "If Jesus had never lived, or if faith in him were shown to be a misunderstanding of the significance of the historical Jesus, then clearly the ground would be taken from under Christian faith."[5] The aim of these men is, therefore, a limited one. They hope to show by historical criticism that there is no break, contradiction, or misunderstanding that divides the Christ of faith, who is preached in the church, from Jesus as he lived in history.

The new quest attempts to learn from the nineteenth century and to avoid the pitfalls into which the first quest fell. The new quest frankly aims to validate the church's faith in Christ as the Lord and Savior, whereas the old quest very frequently was motivated with a desire to discredit the faith of the church.

Although Bultmann concedes that the new quest differs from the old, he has been sharply critical of it.[6] He believes that it has failed and must fail in its goal. He argues that we cannot demonstrate more than that there is a continuity between the historical Jesus and the fact that a kerygma was preached. That is, because Jesus lived, we have a church preaching that God has made him Lord and Savior. The new quest has wanted to do more than this. It wants to show that the faith preached by the church is what it is because Jesus was what he was. But, argues Bultmann, this is impossible because the Christ of the kerygma, the Son of God, who died for man's sins and was raised for our salvation, could not "enjoy continuity with the historical Jesus."[7]

Bultmann's disciples who have inaugurated the new quest for the historical Jesus have not been able to reach agreement upon what Jesus truly was like in history.[8] But the confusion is even more confounded because the new quest has been taken up by another group that does not take its starting point from Bultmann. In it are men like Ethelbert Stauffer, Herman Diem, Paul Althaus, and

Joachim Jeremias. The reader can compare the two forms of the new quest by reading Gunther Bornkamm's *Jesus of Nazareth* and Ethelbert Stauffer's *Jesus and His Story*.

The second school of the new quest differs from the first in both its theological presuppositions and in its historical methods. Theologically, the first school is content if it can demonstrate that the historical Jesus does not contradict the church's faith in Christ. For example, this school does not believe that it is necessary to demonstrate that Jesus presented himself as an object of faith—the Messiah. It is sufficient to show that he had a sense of being uniquely called, and that he proclaimed a time of eschatological decision. On theological grounds, the second school feels that more must be established. Stauffer, for example, fears that the first school is substituting faith in the church and its proclamation for faith in Jesus Christ. Stauffer argues that it would be illegitimate for the church to claim more for Christ than he claimed for himself. Unless he claimed to be an object of faith, it would be illegitimate for the church to present him as such.[9] Thus, the second school is concerned to show that Jesus did claim to be the Messiah and that he called men to have faith in him.

With regard to historical method, the second school does not agree that it is impossible to write a biography of Jesus. It is not committed so exclusively to the form-critical method as is the first quest. Stauffer is more confident than the first school that historical facts can be reconstructed apart from interpretation.

Has the new quest, in any of its forms, succeeded where the nineteenth-century quest failed? Exponents of the new quest generally seem to believe that they have succeeded. Heinz Zahrnt believes it has demonstrated that "post-Easter faith is no more than the correct understanding of the pre-Easter Jesus."[10] But discontent with the new quest has set in. Braaten and Harrisville point out that already we are at the "end of the beginning of the new quest."[11]

Sometime ago, Braaten asked whether we could expect more from the new quest than from the old. Could we hope that it would produce anything more than a "fluctuating magnitude upon which the historians themselves cannot agree"? Despite the youth of the new quest, Braaten's doubts are justified when we see that the new questers, like the old, come up with different pictures of the real Jesus. Zarhnt says that Stauffer's efforts are no more than "the rear light of a train which left fifty years before."[12] The bystander is bewildered. Stauffer is a qualified historian who, like Zahrnt, is attempting to cast out the demons of historical doubt. But Zahrnt would forbid him to do so "because he was not following us" (Mark 9:38).

The new quest recognizes that the old quest failed because it re-created Jesus in its own image. There is evidence that the new quest is repeating the same blunder. Thus, historian Samuel Laeuchli charges that Ebeling's conclusions make Jesus into "a twentieth century existentialist Lutheran who searches for security."[13] Do we need to add that Ebeling is a twentieth-century existentialist Lutheran who seeks security? Zahrnt asks if Bultmann's well-known radical criticism does not in fact conceal a theological presupposition which leads to the radical nature of his criticism.[14] This is a cogent question, but, of course, Bultmann can quite properly reply by asking if Zahrnt's own historical findings are not affected by *his* theological presuppositions.

It would seem that modern theology has come to an impasse. On the one hand, it recognizes that Christianity is a historical faith, rooted in events that happened. On the other hand, when it attempts to show how faith is related to historical studies there is no agreement. Has Protestantism been freed from the infallible declarations of the pope only to bow meekly before the latest styles and fads of historical specialists? Must faith be suspended until the historians achieve agreement?

The discussion of history and faith seems to have suffered because the term "history" means different things. The debate often operates with the debaters using different meanings. The German distinction between *Historie* and *Geschichte* is not sufficient to bring out all these uses. There are at least four different meanings of history, and all of them seem to be involved in the current theological debate.

The first and basic use of the word "history" is to designate events that have happened. To call something historical is to set it apart from myths, legends, or fiction. It is thus highly confusing when some theologians argue that the resurrection of Jesus was not "a historical event" and yet go on to make it clear that they believe that Jesus was raised from the dead. It is misleading because, to the average man, if something is not a "historical" event, it follows *by definition* that it did not happen. Obviously the theologian is using a different meaning of history.

This basic meaning of history as "that which happened" seems simple, but as we look more closely we find that it hides a host of complexities. In the laboratory the scientist can isolate his experiments and thus tell rather accurately just what happened. But when we deal with the history of man, we find that things become complicated. To know what "really happened" requires that we search for motives, character, and other features that do not intrude on a physicist's experiment. Furthermore, a historical event cannot be isolated in a laboratory setting. Each historical event is related to a host of other events, and unless we see an event in relation to other events, we can seldom say "what happened." To take a very simple example, what happened in yesterday's baseball game cannot be explained adequately unless we know something about the rules of baseball, its past history, the current schedule, and a host of other facts. Many a man has had a frustrating experience of taking his wife to a ball game only to have her ask continually, "What happened?" even when she has watched the whole play in question. Although the man and his wife observed the same events, their reports on what happened would be radically different.

It is in this basic sense of the term "history" that Christianity claims to be a historical faith. It is based on good news and there is no news, good or bad, unless something actually happened. The fact that the church produced four Gospels within about sixty years reveals how important it was to the early Christians to remember what happened.

Like other historical events, those constituting the life of Jesus are complex. To see what really happened we must see them in a broader context. They fit into the story of God and his dealings with the Jews. Furthermore, in history we often cannot know what really happened until we can see the event in the light of its long-range results. The Jesus of history cannot be understood without taking into account the fact that from out of his life there came the Christian Church. The church was born and nourished in the conviction that Jesus was an act of God, the Lord and Savior of mankind. A major flaw in many attempts to discover the historical Jesus is that the Jesus they find is inadequate to explain what we know to be the results of Jesus' life.

Bultmann agrees that Christianity depends upon something that happened. But can we agree with his claim that the Christian is interested only in the fact *that* Jesus has come? Does not the existence of the Gospels make it clear that it is important to know *who* has come? Perhaps, as is often said today, the Gospels are not sufficient material for a biography of Jesus. We cannot use them to work out a detailed chronological account of Jesus' life from the cradle to the grave. But the Gospels narrate a sufficient number of significant stories, so that we get a clear picture of the kind of person that Jesus was.

The importance of the picture of Jesus that is given by the Gospels can be shown by a crude illustration. Suppose that, historically, it became evident that Jesus did not bless little children, but kicked them out of his way; he did not forgive his enemies, but cursed them; he did not chase the money changers out of the Temple, but expropriated one of their tables to make some extra money for himself. In that case, Christian faith would be radically different. If God became man in this child-kicking, enemy-cursing, money changer, we would have to confess that God is radically different from what Christians have proclaimed him to be. If we accept the Christian faith that Jesus Christ is the incarnation of God, then we must take seriously the historical nature of the person of Jesus. We must know more than that a man named Jesus has come.

History means "that which happened," but there is a second use for the word "history." This comes out when we recall that only a small number of the events that occur are remembered. Thus history comes to mean not simply what happened, but "the significant events that happened."

If we say that a man will go down in history, we are predicting that future generations will find this man and his works so significant that they will choose to remember him. As a result, if we say that something is a "historic" event, we normally mean more than that it happened. We mean that this event is a significant happening, one worth remembering.

In recent discussion of the historical value of the Gospels, much has been made of the fact that they are "Interpretations" of the life of Jesus. They were not written, we are told, as pure chronicles of the life of Jesus, they were meant to win men to accept Christ as Lord. This is obviously true, but it does not set the Gospels apart from other historical records in any absolute sense. As Markus Barth points out, no event is seen by all its contemporaries and no event is related unless some of its witnesses judge it significant and thus worth retelling.[15] But, to judge an event as significant is already to put an interpretation upon it. Thus, to say that the Gospels are interpretations is not to say anything very startling. Where can we find a historical record of which this is not true?

Psychology has found that what an individual remembers and forgets gives a deep insight into the nature of the individual in question. Similarly, what a people choose to remember or forget tells much about the people in question. No society wants to remember its complete past. Newspapers paid little attention to Lincoln's Gettysburg Address when it was first delivered, but the United States remembers it as a profound expression of its national life. Obviously the American people have come to interpret the Address differently from the newspapers of Lincoln's time.

All of this means that a profound study of history will never be content to recount certain facts of the past. It

will always seek to understand why these facts were considered so important that they, rather than other facts,
were worthy of remembering. The form-critical method of
historical study has performed a service in reminding us
to look for the reasons why those who told of Jesus chose
to recount the stories which they tell. An account of Jesus
which omitted the fact that he was remembered because
he was believed to have been the risen Lord would be a
distortion of the facts. It would not inform us as to why
this story was considered worth remembering. John Knox
has an important point when he affirms that the meaning
of the event of Jesus is the coming into being of the
church.[16] The history of Jesus is inevitably linked to the
church, because only in the church do we see why Jesus
was remembered.

This second meaning of history comes close to the meaning of the German term *Geschichte*. *Geschichte* is history
that is still alive for the historian; it is history in which the
historian finds meaning for himself. But this does not
mean that history in this sense can be sharply separated
from history in the first sense. What is remembered will
depend upon a people's evaluation of what is significant,
but still we can *remember* only that which has happened.
Form criticism is a valuable tool insofar as it locates certain concerns and needs in the life of the early church
which explain why it remembered and recorded particular
events and sayings from the life of Jesus. But from such
findings, form critics often have drawn the unjustified conclusion that the church probably invented such narratives
to meet its needs. Lincoln's Gettysburg Address obviously
has been remembered because it speaks to certain needs of
the American people, but by no logic does it follow that it
was invented by later Americans to meet those needs.

The word "history" has a third meaning in which it

denotes the study and work of professional historians. The professional historian is almost as old as the human race. Even in primitive tribes there was someone, perhaps the witch doctor, who learned and transmitted the tribal history. In ancient Greece, with men like Herodotus and Thucydides, the professional historian began to be more than a simple repeater of the material that he received. He became a critic weighing the evidence and making judgments as to its value. By the time Plutarch wrote his *Lives* in the first century, he could say, "Let us hope that Fable may, in what shall follow, so submit to the purifying processes of Reason as to take the character of exact history."[17] What the Germans call *Historie* had begun. The historian became one who developed methods to distinguish fact from legend and myth. The so-called higher criticism of the Bible is the application of such methods to the Bible.

During the nineteenth century there was a widespread view that such history was a science. But there seems to be considerable wisdom in the custom of American universities in locating the history department among the humanities. Good history has some scientific aspects but it is always as much of an art as it is a science. The historian is never a mere discoverer of facts, he is also one who must fit facts into a pattern, weigh their significance and relate them to each other meaningfully.

There are several reasons why the historian is as much artist as scientist. He must deal with the unique and the individual, and there cannot be a science of the individual case. Historians are rightly suspicious of the historian who finds all history operating according to certain laws. They are sure that he is forcing the unique events into his preconceived patterns. Of course, there are similarities between events, if there were not there would be no scientific aspect to history, but the most interesting feature of any historical event is its uniqueness.

Because historical events are unique, they cannot be repeated for observation as can the experiments of physical scientists. The historian cannot go back to observe the events that he relates in order to check the reliability of his methods.

Another problem is that the historian is personally involved in history in a way that the chemist is not involved in chemistry. This is why the German distinction between *Historie* and *Geschichte* is positively misleading. Every historian finds that the events he relates come to life in his life, and his relationship to these events colors his retelling of them. A fascinating study of this can be found by comparing histories of the last year of the American Civil War as told from the Northern viewpoint by Bruce Catton in *A Stillness at Appomattox* and Clifford Dowdey's Southern viewpoint as told in *Lee's Last Campaign*. Sometimes it seems that the only thing these two books have in common is the names of the places where battles were fought. A similar case study could be made of the War of 1812, as told in Canadian and United States histories. In such cases we could not decide which of the accounts is correct by getting a historian from Outer Mongolia to write about the events on the theory that he could pass an "objective" judgment. The so-called objective viewpoint in history would not necessarily be superior to that of a man who was involved. It is debatable if any historical event can be understood by a man who does not become involved in it with sympathy and empathy. But, in fact, even the man from Outer Mongolia would become involved. He would have his feelings about the contemporary countries that once were involved in the events and this would affect his historical work. As he studied the past events, he would see parallels with events in which he is personally involved and this would color his interpretation.

This is not to imply that there is no difference between history and propaganda. There is a scientific as well as an artistic aspect to history, and the true historian does not sell his soul by rewriting history to fit prejudices. The point is that history is never independent of the historian. As a result, the study of histories is illuminating. It illuminates not only the periods *about* which the histories are written, it also reveals much about the periods *in* which they were written. Anyone who examines the shifting histories of the Cromwellian period in England will see this point. To write history has some parallels with taking a Rorschach test. The historian gives information about himself and his times as well as about his subject.

A fourth meaning of the word "history" is important in the contemporary discussion. This fourth meaning is apparent when, for example, Ebeling asserts that the exclusion of the accounts of the resurrection of Jesus is "a self evident principle" for historical research.[18] Why is this self-evident? If history means that which happened, we cannot say that it is self-evident that the resurrection is not historical. Since the disciples relate it as an event that in fact did happen, we cannot rule it out as self-evidently false, we must investigate to see if the accounts are believable or not. It can hardly be self-evident if by history we mean significant events that have happened. If Jesus rose from the dead, it is obviously most significant. Finally, it cannot be self-evident if, by history, we mean the findings of professional historians, for we can easily find a host of capable historians who argue that we have sufficient historical evidence for believing that the resurrection did occur. It can be self-evident only if we operate with a fourth use of the word "history," and this is what Ebeling is doing.

This use of the word "history" is described by Richard R. Niebuhr when he says, "From the middle of the nineteenth century to the present, the acceptance of the methods of historical criticism has more often than not implied the necessity of also accepting as proven a particular conception of historical causality."[19] This conception of causality has ruled out any event that is not explainable in terms of presently known laws of nature and psychology. In short, it rests upon a particular metaphysical position which is not argued but assumed.

This is made clear by Zahrnt when he says that we can believe that Jesus suffered under Pontius Pilate because we know that other men were crucified under Pilate. But, he continues, to say that "on the third day he arose from the dead" is not to speak of a historical event in the "strict sense of the word," because we do not say that other men rose from the dead.[20]

When a layman hears a historian declare that the resurrection of Jesus is not a historical event, he assumes that the historian has collected historical evidence that demonstrates the falsity of the accounts that tell us that Jesus did rise. But if the layman looks more closely, he will find that usually this is not the case. The historians have not looked at any evidence, because they "knew" before they looked that "in history," dead men stay dead, and that therefore, the Easter story cannot be "historical." History has been rewritten by definition.

These different meanings of the word "history" help to clarify some of the disputes and positions in the contemporary discussion. The man who says that Christian faith has no interest in the historical Jesus is not necessarily divorcing Christian faith from "that which happened." He may simply be arguing that Christian faith cannot wait for professional historians to arrive at a consensus. A man who argues that the resurrection of Jesus is a matter of faith, not history, is not necessarily arguing for wishful thinking. He may simply be saying that it is impossible to prove the resurrection in such a way that all historians, regardless of their metaphysical assumptions, will be convinced. Before we argue with a man's statement about history, we need to analyze what he means to say with it.

There is one conclusion, it would seem, that we can draw from the recent debates on history. All historical judgments are a complex mixture of interpretation and fact. It is only rarely that we can separate the "facts" and then interpret them. The interpretation plays a role in deciding what the facts are. This would seem to be true of all historical judgments, but it is particularly true of the discussion of the historical Jesus.

It is not difficult to see why this is so. Jesus of Nazareth came and forced men to make a decision about how they would interpret him. Some called him the Christ, some called him a prophet, and some called him a blasphemer. Today this same Jesus is proclaimed by the church as Lord, and in the light of the proclamation, men must still decide how they will interpret him. The failure of the search for the historical Jesus to come to any consensus indicates that we cannot first get the facts and then make our interpretation. Our interpretation will color the facts we accept.

The man who begins from the interpretation of Jesus

that sees him as an ordinary man will not be convinced by the stories of his resurrection. The man who begins from a place where he believes that the living Christ has met him in the church will find the same stories convincing as narratives of what "really happened." Such a man may find the quest for the "historical Jesus" to be irrelevant, since he believes that the pages of the New Testament present to him Jesus as he was in history.

The relationship of faith and history will no doubt continue to plague Christian thought. Because it is rooted in historical events, Christianity must make the attempt to weigh the validity of its historical sources. Because the sources present the picture of one who demanded and still demands a decision, any man's historical conclusions will be deeply colored by the interpretations with which he begins. The layman in this field is not at the mercy of the experts for the simple reason that both must make their decision about how they will interpret Jesus. Faced by the disagreement of the experts, the layman cannot escape the need to make his own decisions.

When God became man, he entered into all the limitations of human life, which means that he also entered the limitations of history. He who would try to "save" the faith from this kind of historical limitation is trying to tear asunder what God himself has joined together. The Christian is by no means asked to leap in the dark, but he is called to make his decision within the framework of history where there are no absolute answers.

CHAPTER IV

The New Face of Conservatism

In the second and third decades of this century, American Christianity was torn by the fundamentalist-modernist controversy. This cleavage was a traumatic shock to American Christianity. The relationship of Christian to Christian is still under the shadow of suspicions that linger on from this battle. Nonfundamentalist Protestants are more likely to hold ecumenical conversation with Roman Catholics than with their fellow Protestants, whose roots lie in fundamentalism. This is illustrated by a recent book called *Living Options in Protestant Theology*. Although the book carefully includes all possible options—even some that do not seem to have much life left in them—it does not include any that are representative of fundamentalism or "orthodoxy." The author explains this by saying, "There are special assumptions and problems operative in orthodox Protestantism that render it also not directly accessible to those who have been nurtured in the atmosphere of liberalism."[1] When one recalls that liberalism proudly boasts of its "open mind" in religion, this confession of the failure of liberalism to look objectively at orthodoxy reveals the traumatic scars of the earlier controversy.

One of the tragic results of the fundamentalist-modernist controversy was the fate of fundamentalism. It met defeat after defeat during the twenties and early thirties. It lost its hold on major denominations and withdrew to form splinter groups that continued to subdivide as fundamentalist fought fundamentalist. Its scholarship became barren and parochial, fighting battles on esoteric fronts that concerned no one else. In the wider theological world, fundamentalism lost all status. It was regarded as extinct as the buffalo, although, like the buffalo, it was preserved on a few reservations for curiosity seekers. Theologians were vaguely aware that parish ministers still had to meet fundamentalists, but this was explained as due to the time lag involved when knowledge filters down to the masses. Theologically speaking, fundamentalism was pronounced dead, and it was assumed that it would soon disappear from its sanctuaries in the hinterlands.

To those who were writing the obituaries of fundamentalism there were a few disturbing signs. Fundamentalist congregations, often drawn from lower-income groups, normally raised more money per capita than liberal congregations. While it was not often mentioned in public, most seminary professors were aware that fundamentalist congregations were providing far more than their share of candidates for the ministry and for mission work. Furthermore, fundamentalists refused to disappear. Instead of joining the dinosaurs in the museum, they grew continually in numbers. During the fifties, American church membership grew at record rates. Year after year the percentage of Americans who belonged to churches set new records. But when the figures were broken down, it became evident that much of the growth was provided by the more conservative and fundamentalist churches. The more liberal forms of Protestantism often fell behind the population growth rate.

While such factors might cast doubt on forecasts of the death of fundamentalism, they could not bring it back into theological respectability. Nonfundamentalist theologians might concede that fundamentalists could inspire commitment, but they still were convinced that fundamentalists had Neanderthal minds. During the fifties, however, a group of young scholars arose from the fundamentalist circles to forge a new theology. These scholars rejected the term "fundamentalist" because they felt that it had become a term of abuse, and not a meaningful description of a theological position. Furthermore, they were conscious of the shortcomings of their theological fathers and wished to remold the tradition. They were as concerned as the liberals of an earlier day were to make Christianity relevant to the modern age, but they were determined not to repeat what they saw as the errors of liberalism. Although most of these young men came from fundamentalist seminaries and colleges, they began taking graduate degrees at nonfundamentalist institutions. They returned to their denominations and seminaries to revitalize the theology that had hardened during the fundamentalist-modernist controversy.

There is no agreed name for this group of scholars. Naturally they have been called "neo-fundamentalist," but any use of the term "fundamentalist" is distasteful to the group. They prefer the name "evangelicals" or "new evangelicals." But other protestants feel that "evangelicals" is a term that should be applied to all protestants and not to one theological school. Many of the group prefer the term "orthodox," and there is much to commend this term, for the group seeks to rediscover and reexpress the orthodox faith of the church. But orthodox is best used as an adjective, so that we need to ask, "An orthodox what?" This question is not facetious; within the group in question one finds orthodox Presbyterians, Baptists, Lutherans, Free Methodists, Mennonites, Episcopalians, and members of more recently founded denominations. Sooner or later the group must face the implicit tensions that are involved in trying to express orthodoxy from such differing concepts of what is orthodox.

In many ways, the best descriptive title for this group is "new conservative." A conservative is one who is marked by the desire to preserve the truth and values of the past, but his mind is not closed to change if he can be persuaded that the change is for the better. The use of the term "conservative" helps to distinguish this group from a movement that can still be called fundamentalist. This latter group is the "radical right" of the theological world, and it is often allied with the radical right of the political world. The distinction between the contemporary fundamentalist movement and the new conservatives is made evident by the fact that the fundamentalists reserve some of their most bitter attacks for the new conservatives.

The reasons for calling this movement conservative can be illustrated by A. Berkley Mickelsen's *Interpreting the Bible*. Mickelsen is conservative, but he is not reactionary. Like Bultmann, he is concerned with the hermeneutical problem—how can we interpret the Biblical text for modern man? He insists that theology must continually change, it must be flexible and directed to the questions that are raised by its age. Too many theologies are answers to questions that men used to ask. On the other hand, he insists that interpretations of the Scripture must be interpretations and not what modern man would have said if he had been writing the Bible. Mickelson respects those who disagree with him and deplores those who treat anyone who disagrees as an opponent "to be run out of town as quickly as possible."[2]

The new conservatives in America have found support from such European writers as G. C. Berkouwer and G. W. Bromiley. Many have found support in the philosophy of Herman Dooyeweerd, the Dutch jurist and philosopher.[3] The journal *Christianity Today* has given the group a voice that is heard by a large proportion of the Protestant clergy. Evangelist Billy Graham represents the movement in the wider life of the church.

Riley Case locates the beginnings of the new conservatism in three books beginning with Carl Henry's *The Uneasy Conscience of Modern Fundamentalism* in 1947 and continuing with the American Scientific Affiliation's *Modern Science and the Christian Faith* and E. J. Carnell's *An Introduction to Christian Apologetics* in 1948.[4] Case has made a good choice of books to illustrate the early beginnings and continuing concerns of the movement.

Carl Henry's book was sharply critical of the ethical stance of earlier fundamentalism. Fundamentalism, he charged, had neglected its obligations to society; it had come to mean not simply a particular theology but also a puritanical form of personal ethics. Although Henry's book was one of the first expressions of the new conservatism, the ethical concern has not been developed since as thoroughly as other concerns.

The American Scientific Affiliation is a scientific group with a theological concern. To become a member, one must have a doctorate in one of the sciences from an accredited school and accept the Bible as God's infallible revelation. The significance of this group appears when we recall the sorry record that was made by earlier fundamentalism in its relationship to science. The group's existence witnesses to the possibility of being both a scientist and a conservative Christian. These scientific allies, however, have not simply supported conservatism; they have stimulated the new conservatives to rethink the whole question of science and religion. No subject has received more attention as the conservative theologians have worked out a variety of ways to relate science and the Bible. Even evolution, once the ultimate heresy to the fundamentalists, has been accepted in some form by most conservatives.

Although Carnell's book on apologetics has many limitations from the point of view of his later work, it was a major attempt to converse with modern philosophy and nonconservative theology. Carnell served warning that the new conservative was no longer content to hide in an intellectual ghetto. He was prepared to march out into the modern world and meet it on its own terms. Today most conservative writings bristle with references to nonconservative theologians, but one seldom finds any reference to the conservatives in the work of nonconservatives. To date, the conversation has been a monologue. Perhaps the time has come to ask which side has the "open mind" today.

The new conservatives have shown a willingness to learn from nonconservative theology and to change their position. For example, there is the shift in their attitude toward the higher criticism of the Bible. In 1948, Carnell argued that conservatives gladly accept lower criticism, the search for the most reliable Biblical texts; but they reject higher criticism, the application of secular historical methods to the study of the Scriptures. He argued that the fundamental presupposition of the higher critic "is that the Bible is just another piece of human writing, . . . not realizing that the Bible's message stands pitted in judgment against that very method itself."[5] By 1959, Carnell was ready to concede that orthodoxy can accept any investigation that throws light on the Scriptures, including that of higher criticism, so long as it "does not involve clear contradiction of the Bible's own testimony."[6] By 1963, however, Mickelsen can say that "historical criticism is an important study and should be supported and encouraged by all students of the Bible." He simply warns that when such study is controlled by a framework of "naturalistic assumptions and philosophical aprioris, the results of painstaking historical investigation are vitiated."[7]

One of the central ideas of fundamentalism was that there is a hard core of doctrine that must be believed if a man is to be saved or be a Christian. The new conservative is very much concerned with true doctrine, but he refuses to identify its acceptance with salvation. For example, E. J. Carnell has distinguished between the place of doctrine in sanctification and in justification. A man is justified, brought into the true relationship with God, through faith alone and not by correct beliefs. But as he grows in the sanctified life of a Christian, he will come to accept more and more correct doctrine. More recently, Carnell has pointed out that the New Testament church did not excommunicate men for false doctrine. Although Paul was shocked by the Corinthians who denied the resurrection, "he did not command the Corinthians to undertake heresy proceedings."[8]

When we think of fundamentalism or conservatism, we are likely to think of the doctrine of the inerrancy of Scripture. The new conservatives have been deeply concerned with this doctrine. On the one hand, they have argued for the inerrancy of Scripture, when properly interpreted, but on the other hand, they often have been critical of the older fundamentalist interpretations. There is a widespread tendency for the group to agree with Billy Graham when he says that acceptance of the deity of Christ is the ground for Christian fellowship and not acceptance of the verbal inspiration of Scripture. Whereas the old-style fundamentalist argued that to deny the truth of any statement of Scripture is to call God a liar, the conservative is more inclined to argue that the man who denies inerrancy falls into contradiction or confusion. Furthermore, from its beginnings, conservatism has emphasized that there are errors in all manuscripts of the Scriptures that we now possess. Only the first manuscripts of the Bible, which are lost, were without error. The conservative simply affirms that the Holy Spirit did not allow any errors in the copying of Scripture that would imperil man's salvation.

The problem that haunts the conservatives is to locate the inerrancy which they claim for the Bible. Carnell created considerable stir when he found "progressive revelation" in the Bible. Fundamentalists, he said, made the mistake of thinking that because the whole Bible is inspired, it must all be equally normative. But, argues Carnell, this does not follow—the Christian needs hermeneutic principles that will enable him to interpret some parts of the Bible in the light of other parts. Thus he argues that the New Testament interprets the Old Testament, the Epistles interpret the Gospels, systematic passages interpret incidental passages on the same subject, and passages of prose teaching interpret the symbolic passages.[9] These principles lead Carnell to the conclusion that since Romans and Galatians are the only places where justification is dealt with systematically, they are the basic norm through which the whole Bible is to be read. This has led to the charge that Carnell has produced an infallible "Bible" within the Bible.

Although Carnell's position has not won the following of all conservatives, it is typical of the new look that conservatives are giving to the doctrine of Scriptural inerrancy. Conservatives have spent considerable time finding Biblical passages that contradict each other in various minor details to show that inerrancy does not mean that every detail of Scripture, as we now have it, is without error. Conservatives argue that the Bible does not answer scientific questions, and sometimes they distinguish between what the Scripture writer *believed* about science and what he *taught*. The claim of the conservative is that the Bible is an inspired and inerrant authority in the realm of faith and doctrine.

In general, the conservative uses three arguments for his position.[10] First, the Bible represents itself as an inspired book. The prophets say, "Thus saith the Lord," and when Biblical books refer to other Biblical books, they presuppose that they are referring to inspired authorities. The conservative does not suppose that he can prove that the Bible is inerrant by quoting it, but he does believe that any honest approach to the Bible must at least take seriously the claim that it makes for itself. Secondly, the conservatives point to the witness of the Holy Spirit in the life and experience of men. As we read the Bible, God himself witnesses to its truth. Thirdly, conservatives point to the history of the church. Through the centuries it has been nourished and strengthened by its belief that God was speaking to it through the Scriptures. On the other hand, many conservatives point to the chaotic condition of modern theology as an object lesson in what happens when theologians abandon belief in the inerrancy of Scripture.

It has been evident for some time that the new conservatives have had difficulties with their concept of inerrancy. On the one hand, their willingness to admit errors in all existing manuscripts of the Bible and to admit that the Bible does not speak inerrantly upon all subjects make them look like modernists to the fundamentalist. But their determination to keep the slogan of inerrancy often closes the doors to conversation with nonconservative theologians who are likely to take a dim view of any doctrine of inerrancy. To both the fundamentalist and the nonconservative, it often seems that the new conservative is trying to say, "The Bible is inerrant, but of course this does not mean that it is without errors."

This implicit contradiction in the new conservatism was met head on by Dewey M. Beegle's book *The Inspiration of Scripture.* Beegle stands within the conservative framework, having been ordained an elder of the Free Methodist Church, graduated from Asbury Theological Seminary, and served as a professor at The Biblical Seminary in New York. Furthermore, he makes it clear that he intends to defend the conservative position. But he insists that conservatives ought not to advocate a doctrine of plenary inspiration or of the inerrancy of the Scriptures.

Beegle argues that conservatives have been misled by a "deductive" approach. They have begun with the assertion that God is perfect and from this they have deduced that God must give a perfect revelation. A perfect revelation could not have any errors. Therefore, it is deduced, since the Scriptures are God's revelation, they must be inerrant. And, notes Beegle, the deductive approach had to go further. The conservatives were forced to admit that we have many manuscripts of the Bible which often differ from one another, they cannot all be inerrant. Thus the conservatives had to deduce that the original manuscripts, now lost, must have been inerrant.

Beegle suggests that this whole attempt to deduce from a definition of God's perfection is unjustified. Instead of such deduction, we ought to take the inductive approach, we ought to examine how God, in fact, has chosen to inspire the Scriptures. When, in this spirit, we turn to the Bible, we find that it teaches that Scripture is authoritative and inspired, but it does not claim inerrancy for itself. When Jesus and the New Testament writers appealed to Scripture, they appealed to the errant copies of their time and not to the supposed inerrant originals. Beegle concludes: "Is one justified . . . in claiming more than Scripture does? Can there be in actuality a higher view than the Biblical view?"[11]

Beegle also argues that the doctrine of inerrancy, in its modern form, is a late doctrine in the history of the church. Through history the church has recognized a divine and a human element in Scripture without precisely systematizing their relationship. The idea of inerrancy has emerged out of the insecurity of modern Christians who are afraid that if the Bible is wrong on anything, it can be trusted in nothing. Beegle finds this to be illogical. In fact, we find that the Bible teaches clearly and unequivocally certain basic truths and it witnesses to the reality of certain basic facts. It also contains much material that is irrelevant to God's purpose, and its writings tend to blend into the noninspired at certain points rather than being sharply distinguished at all points from non-Biblical writings. In God's world a high degree of inspiration sometimes occurs outside of Scripture and a low level within, but this does not change the fact that the Scriptures, as a whole, are essential to God's revelation of himself to man.

Beegle hopes to institute a conversation between conservative and nonconservative theologians. He feels that semantics has often kept the two groups from understanding each other. Conservatives have been concerned to argue that the Bible is God's revelation whether any man accepts it or not. But in saying this, they have run the danger of equating faith with believing certain doctrines taught in the Scriptures. To combat this, neo-orthodoxy has emphasized that faith is a trustful commitment to God revealed in Christ. Revelation is thus not something printed on a page; it occurs when the Holy Spirit inspires the reader to see God at work through the words of Scripture. Beegle believes that neo-orthodoxy has rescued the Biblical meaning of faith, but it is in danger of overlooking the importance of propositional truths. After all, Jesus was known as a teacher and the Bible puts great emphasis upon teaching. Without words of explanation, for example, Jesus' death would have been a complete enigma to the disciples.

Beegle likens the contemporary debate between conservative and neo-orthodox theologians to the old conundrum, "Would there be sound if a tree fell where there was no ear to hear the fall?" Insofar as "sound" implies airwaves, we can say that there would be sound even if no one heard it. But, insofar as "sound" also implies an ear that transforms the airwaves into the experience of sound, we can say that without an ear, the falling tree would cause no sound. To argue the point is fruitless because it revolves around how we want to use the word "sound."

As Beegle sees it, those who want to say that the Bible is God's revelation regardless of whether men accept it or not are like those who argue that there is sound in the woods even though no one hears it. On the other hand, those who insist that Scripture becomes the Word of God only as it is witnessed to by the Holy Spirit in the heart of the reader, are like those who argue that there is no sound if there is no one to hear. The two groups can come to mutual understanding if they will only see that revelation, like all communication, involves three elements. There is the communicator or source; there is the message; and there is the response of the receiver. When any of the three are missing, there is no communication. Conservatives rightly stress the Book as the givenness of God's message. Neo-orthodoxy has rightly insisted that before revelation is complete it must be received. The two approaches do not contradict each other; they complement each other.

The real problem, believes Beegle, is the question of the historical nature of the events that form the basis for faith. Christian faith can live with a recognition that the Scriptures contain errors in minor details of its history, but it cannot live without believing that the "key events" in which God reveals himself and saves man are truly factual. Here, he believes that Bultmann's skepticism about such facts undermines the faith. To take up his former analogy, it would seem that Beegle believes that Bultmann is saying that it does not matter if the tree fell or not just so long as you can hear it fall. The attempt of Bultmann to rest faith in the preaching of the church and not in historical facts fails, believes Beegle, because as Brunner says, "The question, What is told us? cannot be separated from that other question, What has happened? for what we are told is precisely that this event has actually happened."[12] Thus Beegle argues that Christianity stands or falls with the factual nature of the resurrection. Furthermore, although belief in the virgin birth is not made central in the New Testament, Beegle argues that where it is doubted, something goes out of the urgency of faith. Men may be saved who doubt the virgin birth, but churches that doubt it have been prone to lose their sense of mission and ability to win men to commitment and sacrifice.

Beegle's book has brought forth considerable criticism from conservative sources. *Christianity Today* dedicated some seven pages to answering it.[13]

Carl Henry, although conceding that inerrancy is not taught by Scripture and that belief in it is not necessary to salvation, nonetheless charged that Beegle has been more precise in saying what he does not believe about inspiration than in saying what he does believe. Henry agrees that man is not saved by doctrine but insists that conservatives have never said that he was. What conservatives do insist is that "there are revealed truths or doctrines, and this Beegle denies." Henry goes on to affirm that "the Creator who fashioned human nature as wholly serviceable to the Incarnation also fashioned human speech as a wholly serviceable medium of divine revelation and inspiration."[14] Beegle desires to communicate the faith without the unnecessary roadblock of belief in Scriptural inerrancy, but Henry argues that this is not a roadblock. The men who believe in inerrancy are the ones who are winning the unbelievers; it is only those who already believe that are persuaded by denials of inerrancy. Despite the attack upon Beegle, it cannot be denied that he represents an important shift in the total pattern of conservatism. Time alone will tell whether the future of conservatism lies with Beegle or Henry.

The argument might be made that the new conservative, even if he does not go all the way with Beegle, has modified his position to the point where he is indistinguishable from the main line of nonconservative theology. But the conservative believes that he has some important points to add to contemporary theology, particularly in the realm of revelation and the relationship of Christianity to science.

The main line of Protestant theology in recent years has insisted that revelation is the revelation of God, and not of propositional truths about God. To use Brunner's much-quoted statement, "What God reveals is God." As John Baillie put it, "When I trust somebody, or have *fiducia* in him, I am manifestly at the same time believing certain things about him to be true, yet I may find it very difficult to say exactly what these things are."[15] Thus, Baillie can argue that Christians first had faith in Christ and then only slowly worked out the intellectual implications of this as various heresies arose to challenge the faith. Such an approach has emphasized "the mighty acts of God" as the primary revelation. In these acts, God has revealed his self to man and called man to response. The Scriptures are the record of the acts in which God manifested himself and they are the record of the human response to the acts of God. Revelation occurs when man today, reading the Scripture, is confronted by God and makes his response under the inspiration of the Holy Spirit.

Conservatives have been ready to learn from this approach to revelation. Thus Kenneth Kantzer agrees that "the ultimate goal of revelation is not so much to make

man wise as it is to bring him into a direct encounter with
God as a person, and to evoke from him a response of love
and obedience to God."[16] Furthermore, Kantzer affirms
that revelation is through divine acts and culminates in
Christ. All of this may be taken as a debt that conservatism is ready to acknowledge to neo-orthodoxy. But Kantzer goes on to insist that revelation is not complete without
interpretation. If God acts, it is still necessary for God to
interpret the meaning of his act. Thus, argues Kantzer,
"The God of most contemporary theologians can act but
does not speak."[17] The conservative maintains that the
Bible contains not only the history of the events in which
God acted, but also the inspired interpretation of the
events and this is why the Bible is the sole means of revelation.

There is a second point on which the new conservatives
feel that they bring a corrective word to modern theology.
They feel that modern theology has tended to adopt the
"modern scientific world view" without criticism. Thus
Mickelsen argues that "those who take seriously the basic
emphases of Scripture must insist that faith offers a much-
needed corrective to the modern scientific world-view."[18]
This is by no means an attempt to reinstitute the old
fundamentalist war with science. The conservative is careful to distinguish between a "scientific world view" and
a "scientific finding." The fundamentalists erred in attempting to argue with the findings of science and this
resulted in discrediting theology. But a "world view" cannot be a finding of science, it is rather a metaphysical
position erected without scientific support. It results from
taking the legitimate operating method of science and
turning it into an illegitimate world view. Because science
must continually try to explain every event in terms of its

causal relations with other events, the "scientific world view" assumes that the whole of reality is contained within the causal nexus that is explainable by science.

A crucial aspect of the conservative's attack on the scientific world view is his defense of the reality of miracles. The conservative does not see a miracle as a breaking of the laws of nature, but as an act of God's freedom. The question is not whether natural laws can be broken, but whether or not God is imprisoned by his own creation. In criticism of Bultmann, Mickelsen says: "Bultmann has a universe with a lid on. Unfortunately one gets the uncomfortable feeling that not only is man shut up to existence under this lid but so is God."[19] Miracles are believed impossible, says Mickelsen, when we assume that our own experience is the only possible experience of any other person or persons on this planet. "Without openness of mind, there is no way for self-correction to root out distortions."[20]

Rachel King presents the conservative position in a critique of Reinhold Niebuhr's theology. She is not always a reliable guide to Niebuhr's thought, but she does express forcefully the conservative position on a scientific world view and miracles. As she understands Niebuhr, he has sold out to a scientific world view and has no room for miracles. But he faces a dilemma. The ethic that he teaches presupposes a righteous God. But if God did not raise his Son from the dead, God is not righteous. "If God allowed Jesus as an individual to die permanently on Good Friday then God has not even the moral decency of the very human masters in Jesus' parables who lavishly reward their faithful servants."[21]

Furthermore, argues Miss King, Niebuhr teaches and needs the doctrine of justification through faith alone as a basis for his ethics. But his world view leaves no room for the Holy Spirit to work within men, which means that man has to save himself by his own efforts after all.

Miss King is typical of the conservative position which is convinced that if theology eliminates miracles it must be reduced to an ethical system. But, as such, it will lack both the direction and power for its ethical ideals. To deny miracles is to deny a living God and to deny a living God is to undermine the foundations of a Christian ethic.

Theology has a way of moving in a circle around certain basic themes. The battles at the center of theology in one generation move to the periphery in another, but a third generation restores them to the center again. Nonetheless, history never simply repeats itself and sometimes, as an old issue is revived, there is a strange realignment of the parties involved. This is true of the discussion of faith and history. In the preceding chapter we saw that this issue, including the search for the historical Jesus, has been revived in our time. But when we examine the position of the conservatives in this debate we find an interesting realignment.

The nineteenth-century search for the historical Jesus was primarily the work of theological liberals and of men who denied Christian faith. During the fundamentalist-modernist controversy, liberalism hailed the search for the historical Jesus as one of its defining characteristics. In a parody of an old gospel hymn, liberals charged that fundamentalism presented only the Christ of the "Cradle, Cross and Tomb." That is, the liberals charged, fundamentalism emphasized only the virgin birth, the substitutionary atoning death, and the resurrection of Christ. Liberals, however, in their search for the historical Jesus were restoring the whole life of Jesus to the preaching of the church. If the issue were to be reexpressed in the modern jargon, we would say that the fundamentalists preached only the "kerygmatic Christ," while the liberals preached the "Jesus of history."

Today, however, as the issue of history again comes to the theological front, the conservatives seem to be rooting for the new quest for the historical Jesus. Carl Henry, in his study of contemporary European theology, argues that one of the reasons why Barth's theology failed to stem the tide of Bultmannian thought was because Barth had failed to ground his thought on objectively discernible historical facts.[22] Although Henry does not feel that the new quest for the historical Jesus has gone far enough, he obviously believes that it is moving in the right direction. Most conservatives defend the historical nature of the gospel records.

As a contribution to the current debate, *Christianity Today* republished J. G. Machen's "History and Faith," which he delivered as his inaugural address in Princeton Theological Seminary in 1915. This address is noteworthy for several reasons. It is a good summary of the contemporary conservative position on this subject. Although it is now fifty years old, it reads very much as though it were written to meet the issues of today, which reminds us that the "latest thinking" is never quite as original as it hopes to be. Finally, the article throws light on why the conservatives of today are defending the search for the historical Jesus.

Machen's article begins by affirming that the Bible is "primarily a record of events," not "eternal ideas."[23] He then goes on to make it clear that he is not opposed to the attempt to discover the Jesus of history because Christian faith is rooted in Jesus. What Machen is opposed to is the picture of Jesus presented by the liberal theologians. As he sees it, the issue is clear-cut. The Jesus who lived in history as the Bible pictures him is a savior who comes from God to deliver man from sin. "The historical Jesus" presented by the liberal theologians is a product of this world, a teacher and an example.

Machen, a New Testament scholar and historian, met the historian's challenge on historical grounds. He argued that the liberal attempt to find the "Jesus of history" had failed. It failed because it could claim no historical justification for its rejection of the "supernatural" portions of the Gospels. The historical records that tell about supernatural miracles have as much grounding in the historical records as the stories that the liberals chose to accept. Machen thus charges that the liberals reconstructed the history of Jesus on the basis of a theological decision, and not on the basis of historical evidence.

The quest also failed, Machen affirms, because, the liberal Jesus is a "monstrosity." He was a humble human teacher and yet he had a Messianic complex. Only by doing the greatest of violence to the historical record can we deny that Jesus claimed to be the Messiah and yet, for the liberal Jesus to do this, he must have been a madman.

Thirdly, the "quest" failed because its Jesus failed to explain the beginning of the Christian church. Jesus, in his lifetime, was not very successful. When he died he had only a handful of disciples, and they did not understand him. And yet these same disciples went out to conquer the Roman world. "Now it seems exceedingly unnatural that Jesus' disciples could thus accomplish what he had failed to accomplish."[24] We know that they were inferior to Jesus in spiritual discernment, they could not understand him, they showed not the slightest trace of originality, and after his death they lost what little courage they had. "How could they institute the mightiest religious movement in the world?" Machen answers his own question, "Christianity never was the continuation of the work of a dead teacher."

But where the liberal "historical Jesus" fails, Jesus as we find him pictured in the Gospels can make sense of what we know to be the history of the church. If he truly did what the Gospels tell us and if he was raised from the dead, then we do not need to do violence to our historical sources; we do not have an insane man with a Messiah complex but the true Messiah, and we can see how the risen Lord was the power behind the spread of the early church.

In short, Machen was, in his own sense, a seeker after the Jesus of history. But, on the basis of historical argument, he believed that he could demonstrate that the Jesus who lived in history was "the Jesus of the Bible." The new conservative's interest in the new quest for the historical Jesus is not completely paradoxical, since it can be seen in continuity with Machen's thought. Nonetheless, as we examine the fruits of the new quest it is apparent that they bear most of the weaknesses that Machen found in the first quest.

Machen's historical concern helps us to see why conservative sympathies tend to lie with the new quest for the historical Jesus. But there is another aspect to his article which does make the theological realignment confusing. After making his historical case, Machen asks: "But how can the acceptance of an historical fact satisfy the longing of our souls? Must we stake our salvation upon the intricacies of historical research?"[25] Machen goes farther when he admits that if faith stops at a historical argument, "it probably never will withstand the fires of criticism." But historical evidence is not alone. This is not a matter of the past; if Christ arose, he is alive today and meets the man of faith. This meeting is the Christian's assurance. And here Machen, the defender of orthodoxy, sounds strangely like Barth or even Bultmann. Theology makes strange bedfellows, especially as the years pass.

The prediction of the future is always a precarious business. Those who confidently forecast the theological death of fundamentalism have been only partially correct. From the tomb of fundamentalism, there has emerged a new conservatism. It has developed considerably in the last fifteen years and shows evidence of continuing to develop. Will the acids of modernity so corrode the young leaders of this movement that they will lose all vital relationship to the faith of their immediate fathers and become simply a slightly conservative expression of modern theology in general? Will this movement produce the real inheritors of Barth's theology? Will the leftward swing of Protestant theology in general leave a vacuum in the theological center that will be filled by the new conservatism? Will the new conservatives prove to be closer to the laity and its problems, so that, while other theologians continually talk about "being relevant," the new conservatives will be relevant? Or, are the new conservatives but the "Indian summer" of fundamentalism, the last burst of color before the leaves fall and the snows bring death? A case could be made for each of these possibilities. Perhaps each will be fulfilled in certain members of the movement. Whatever be the future, the new conservatives have restored intellectual life to the theological right.

CHAPTER V

Sanctification Rediscovered

An important development in recent theology is a renewal of interest in sanctification. The theological analysis of Christian salvation is often divided into justification and sanctification. Justification deals with how a man becomes a Christian. It describes God's forgiving acceptance of the sinner and the sinner's response of faith. Sanctification is the act of God whereby the forgiven man is made righteous, it describes how a man grows in his Christian life. Although for the purposes of analysis these may be separated, in actual life they cannot be sharply separated. When a man accepts God's forgiving love he trusts God and puts his life into God's hands.

The contemporary theological concern with sanctification has come at an appropriate time because the church today is facing widespread criticism of its life and practice. During the fifties of this century, the church in America sailed on a wave of popular approval. As church membership rose to all-time heights, a moratorium was called on any serious criticism of the church. The man who raised reservations about the church was likely to be called a communist. The only charges against the churches that could hope to be respectable were those which claimed that the churches had been infiltrated by communists. But it is significant that in the end these attacks did more to discredit the attackers than they did to harm the church. The church had little to fear from its critics. But, happily for the sake of the church's soul, those days have passed.

Today a growing number of voices are raised in criticism of the church. These voices are not raised primarily against the faith of the church, but rather against its practices. Rolf Hochhuth's play *The Deputy* is typical of this criticism. This play rocked two continents by launching a scathing criticism of Pope Pius' failure to protest Nazism's slaughter of six million Jews. Protestants had no time to take any unholy glee in the discomfiture of their Catholic brethren because criticism was being directed at the Protestant Church also.

Newspapers carried a fascinating story in March of 1964, telling of President Johnson's address to a group of Southern Baptist ministers. Johnson took the occasion to preach a rousing sermon in which he called the church to accept its responsibility in the racial crisis. Protestant churches have prided themselves on being the conscience of the state, but here, ironically, the representative of the state was acting as the conscience of the church.

For many years, the Negro meekly asked the churches to do something about racial discrimination. But today the Negro is saying, in effect: "We are going to win our freedom. You may join us or not but tomorrow it will be too late. We shall no longer need you."

Folk songs, which have been enjoying great popularity, are noted for their pungent criticism of all sacred cows. Recently their barbs have frequently been aimed at the church. An English folk song parodies a bishop who blesses the hydrogen bomb and counsels that it be dropped "with love" on the enemy. Bonnie Dobson, a Canadian folk singer, comments that we have heard a great deal about putting Christ back into Christmas, but, she suggests, it would suit her if we would just put him back into Christianity.

When one talks to college students today, one finds sharp criticism of the church's failure in the field of ethical leadership. As one student put it after reading Bishop Robinson's plea for a new theology in *Honest to God:* "I don't ask the church to invent a new theology. I just want to see it practice the one it already has."

The Anglican Church in Canada took the daring step of asking Canada's leading agnostic, Pierre Berton, to write a book explaining what he found wrong with the church. The book, *The Comfortable Pew,* has created more stir in Canada than has any other book dealing with religion. Berton had a few predictable things to say about the church's "out-of-date" language and theology, but the core of his criticism was aimed at the church's "abdication of leadership," its failure to call men to a life of Christian action in the world. As Berton sees it, the church has been so afraid of losing people by speaking on controversial issues that it has bored them to death.[1]

In the fall of 1964, a musical opened on Broadway that had been a hit in London, *Oh, What a Lovely War.* There have been few more devastating criticisms of the church's support of war than this production. Often making use of hymn tunes, it presents in vivid contrasts the piety of prayers and the horror of the victories for which the prayers were offered.

These examples illustrate a new spirit of criticism toward the church. It is significant, therefore, that even before this criticism became widespread, theologians were taking a new look at the doctrine of sanctification. Dietrich Bonhoeffer's book *The Cost of Discipleship* was a pioneering work in the field. Emil Brunner, in the third volume of his *Dogmatics,* gives careful attention to sanctification. Tillich's theology has culminated in his doctrine of the New Being, which deals with most of the traditional concerns of sanctification. L. H. DeWolf declares from a liberal perspective that sanctification is the forgotten doctrine. The new conservatives have likewise been concerned with rediscovering sanctification.

Although interest in sanctification is widespread and transcends the theological divisions of the recent past, the major treatment of sanctification in our time has come from Karl Barth. On this continent we have been slow to understand Barth. We have preferred a caricature of his thought which pictured his theology as an otherworldly faith that was irrelevant to the daily life and decisions of man. Barth, we assumed, spoke profoundly about the ultimate issues of God and man, but he had so emphasized sin and salvation through faith alone that he had encouraged an antinomian attitude. Not even Barth's heroic opposition to Nazism was allowed to shake this stereotype. It was argued that this action was not based on his theology; the man was better than his theology. Even on the basis of Barth's early writing, this should have been recognized as a distorted view of his position. But, since the appearance of the fourth volume of his *Dogmatics,* it has become evident that Barth has developed one of the most extensive treatments of sanctification since the work of John Wesley. Far from leading to an antinomian position, Barth says: "What is the forgiveness of sins (however we understand it) if it is not directly accompanied by an actual liberation from the committal of sin? . . . What is faith without obedience?"[2]

The contemporary concern with sanctification needs to be seen in the light of earlier twentieth-century theology in which the doctrine of sanctification was neglected. Liberal theology spoke a great deal about the Christian life and ethics. There were some liberals for whom ethics became the essence of Christianity. The liberal search for the historical Jesus was primarily a search for one who would be an ethical inspiration and leader for men. But an inspiring example is not one who sanctifies, he is one who encourages men to make themselves righteous. Liberals were prophetically scornful of professions of faith that did not issue in ethical living, but they contributed relatively little to a theological understanding of how the Christian might find the power to live the Christian life. Although there were notable exceptions, liberals tended to be optimistic about human nature. They hoped that a combination of evolutionary development, education, reason, ethical exhortation, and an effort by the will of man, would lead to the good life.

One of the first points at which the neo-orthodox theology attacked liberalism was on its doctrine of man. Man, the neo-orthodox theologians declared, was more a slave to sin than liberalism had realized. No combination of ethical exhortation or efforts of man's will could free him from his bondage to sin. These theologians turned to the Bible and found a picture of man's sinful predicament that corresponded to the events of the twentieth century and to the discoveries of depth psychology. Man, they affirmed, was alienated from God and this resulted in a self-centered life of pride. Salvation could not be achieved by man's own efforts; it required the free grace of God's forgiveness. Justification through faith alone was rediscovered.

In the early days of neo-orthodoxy, however, there were few attempts to move beyond justification to a doctrine of sanctification. Rightly or wrongly, the neo-orthodox leaders were interpreted as teaching that salvation means that God forgives the sinner but that sin itself is not overcome. To-day we can see that it was the camp followers who were more guilty of this idea than the theological leaders but even the leaders were so concerned to analyze the sinful-ness of man that they had little time left to speak of the new life. It was against this background that Bonhoeffer spoke out against the dispensing of "cheap grace," which promises forgiveness without calling for the living of a new life.[3]

To understand the current emphasis upon sanctifica-tion, we need to see three of its basic themes. It accepts a basically pessimistic view of human nature, but a highly optimistic view of the power of God's grace; it emphasizes the uniqueness of the Christian ethic; and it recognizes that sanctification must be deeply rooted in the church. We shall examine each of these.

The new concern with sanctification has not arisen from a more optimistic view of human capacities than was held by the earlier neo-orthodox theology. The doctrine of sanc-tification is seen in closest relationship to the doctrine of justification. Man, in his sin, cannot save himself, and even the justified sinner cannot make himself righteous by his own efforts. Whereas many liberals accepted only a moral-influence theory of atonement, the new concern with sanctification almost always presupposed that an ob-jective difference was made in man's relationship to God because Christ bore the price of sin and rose from the dead to defeat the powers of evil. There is a real optimism in this concern for sanctification, but it is an optimism about the grace of God, not about the ability of man.

Consequently, those who have rediscovered sanctifica-tion emphasize that sanctification is as much the work of God's grace as is justification. Barth, for example, repudiates the popular Protestant view that justification is God's forgiving work for man, while sanctification is man's work of gratitude for what God has done. He says that the New Testament "knows nothing of a Jesus who lived and died for the forgiveness of our sins, to free us as it were retrospectively, but who now waits as though with tied arms for us to act in accordance with the freedom achieved for us."[4] Since it is God's grace that operates in sanctification, the Christian has no more reason to boast about his growth in sanctification than he has to boast about his justification.

In a similar fashion, L. H. DeWolf, speaking out of a liberal heritage, argues that justification and sanctification cannot be separated. Faith, he argues, does not free us from ethical requirements. "Rather, the grace of God given through Christ and received by faith enables us to live righteously."[5] DeWolf goes on to draw upon Wesley, who understood sanctification as the other side of the coin from God's act of justifying man.

When the doctrine of sanctification is rooted in God's grace it becomes very different from a mere call to ethical striving or heroism. In classical Christian terms, this is the difference between law and gospel. The law comes to man with a demand, "This you must do!" Quite normally the law is accompanied by promises of reward for good behavior and with threats of punishment for disobedience. Rewards and punishments may be presented in a wide variety of forms, including the traditional pictures of heaven or hell, social approval or disapproval, world peace or atomic disintegration, happiness or unhappiness, mental health or sickness, and so on. The mark of the law is always that it places upon man a demand that must be fulfilled. The word "gospel" means good news, and so the gospel does not come with a demand, it comes with a gift. It does not say, "You must live a good life or else!" It says, "You are given the gift of a good life."

Consequently, Barth says that it is important to see that justification and sanctification together form the one act of God's salvation for man. We can distinguish them by saying that in justification, God forgives man, while in sanctification, God remakes man to live a new life. Furthermore, there is even a kind of priority to justification in that, before a man's life can be changed, he needs to hear that he is forgiven and freed from sin. But Barth fears that if we make too much of this distinction, we may seem to say, "God will justify [i.e., forgive and love] you if you will sanctify your life and become good." This, of course, would be to change the gospel back into a law with a promise and a thinly veiled threat. When Jesus told the woman taken in adultery to go and sin no more, he did not add, "Because the next time I shall let them stone you."

Again, Barth does not want to separate justification and sanctification too sharply because it may lead to the assumption that sanctification is optional for the Christian. He may cling to his forgiveness as "cheap grace" and not worry about obedience to God. Thus Barth wants to emphasize that God does not forgive a man on the condition that he become righteous, but he does forgive man in order that he may become righteous. We might even say that the end and goal of justification is sanctification.[6]

A second feature of the contemporary concern for sanctification is its desire to express the uniqueness of the Christian ethic. This is more striking than it may sound, for Christian history reveals that the church has, in most eras, identified as Christian the "best" ethical thinking of its time and place. Langdon Gilkey has pointed out that the difference between liberal and conservative Christians today is not that one accepts the culture and the other rejects it; the difference is the way in which each of them accepts the same culture.[7] We might add to Gilkey's point that there is some tendency for the more liberal Christians to adopt as Christian the newest ethical insights, while conservative Christians are likely to be defending the best ethics of fifty years ago.

The church's acceptance of the ethical values of its time and place is not to be simply deplored. Liberal Christians have often led their society in bringing new ethical insights to fruition and conservatives have often helped to preserve real values that would have been carelessly tossed aside in the name of "progress." But the fact still remains that a church that becomes too comfortably allied with the "best" ethical thinking of its culture is a church that can no longer bring a real word of judgment to that culture. The exponents of sanctification today are concerned that the church should have something to say to our culture that the culture is not already saying to itself.

As Barth sees it, only a sound doctrine of sanctification enables us to speak of a distinctively Christian ethic. Christ's question, "What do *you* more than others?" is cogent only if the Christian has received the power to do more. Barth's understanding of the Christian life is thus summed up in the English title given to a collection of his essays, *Against the Stream*. For Barth, the sanctified Christian is not called to live a mildly respectable life; he is called to swim against the stream, to witness to God's judgment over every *status quo*. Bonhoeffer made the same point when he said, "For Luther the Christian's worldly calling is sanctified only in so far as that calling registers the final, radical protest against the world."[8]

Barth argues that if the Christian does not have an adequate doctrine of sanctification, he will be forced to find his ethical guidance in something other than the gospel. He may draw a law from the Bible itself, he may use reason to develop a natural law, or he may identify the Christian ethic with his own cultural viewpoint. But what makes the Christian ethic unique is that it is not a law, not even one drawn from the Bible. Here Barth joins Bonhoeffer in identifying discipleship as the key to the Christian life. To be a disciple means to accept Jesus Christ as the Lord of one's life; it means being ready to forsake all to follow him.

When we commit ourselves to being a disciple of Christ, we find, says Barth, that Christ calls us from the things of the world. We find that worldly possessions, worldly honor, the family, the laws of religion, all may become gods that keep us centered on ourselves and thus not open to the redeeming love of God. Thus it is tempting to assume that the only safe way is to flee from the things of the world and to seek refuge in some ascetic monasticism. But, asserts Barth, such a flight to the cloister would be a defeat, not a victory, for Christ. If the Christian cannot live in the world with the things of the world, it implies that they have not been overcome and defeated in Christ. The first task of the Christian is not to save his soul, but to risk it for the sake of God's world.

Although the Christian disciple will live in the world, using the things of the world, he will do it in a way that wins the displeasure of the world. The Christian ought not to antagonize the world, argues Barth. When Daniel was in the lion's den, he did not pull the lion's tail. But, the Christian who remains loyal to Christ can expect the opposition of the world. Nonetheless, he must not think of himself as a warrior crusading against the world. He is not fighting *against* other men; he is fighting *for* them. Instead of fighting against others and adding to their woes, the Christian must be prepared to suffer at their hands, as did Christ.

As an example of the radical ethic of Christian discipleship, Barth looks at the question of the use of force. The disciples "were neither to fear force nor to exercise it."[9] They were not to fear it, because the users of force could only kill the body, not the soul. But those who do not fear force cannot use force against others. How sharply Jesus rebukes his disciples when they want to call down force on a hostile village! (Luke 9:52 f.) Similarly, when a disciple tried to protect Jesus with a sword, Jesus ordered him to put up his sword and warned him that those who take the sword must perish by the sword. (Matt. 26:47 f.) But, believes Barth, Jesus goes deeper still. Force does not begin with killing; it begins with anger in the heart. (Matt. 5:21 f.) Thus, the disciple is called to love his enemy. It would seem that Barth is on the verge of identifying Christianity with pacifism, but he does not, for to do so, he argues, would lead to a new law. It would make a principle or law out of the nonuse of force, so, he affirms, the Christian cannot be a pacifist "on principle." But he goes on to say that "we have to consider very closely whether, if we are called to discipleship, we can avoid being practical pacifists."[10]

The rediscovery of the doctrine of sanctification with its implications for a Christian ethic seems likely to result in a major debate over the whole question of the Christian social ethic. In recent years, at least in America, a sort of "orthodoxy" has emerged in the realm of social ethics. Although frequently associated with the name of Reinhold Niebuhr, it has been preached widely in Protestant circles and often preached in forms that Niebuhr would find crass and undefendable. In general, this position emphasizes that it is impossible to live perfectly in the sociopolitical realm. It repudiates, as "utopian," all attempts to escape from using power and urges the "responsible" use of power. Although it often affirms that "power tends to corrupt; and absolute power tends to corrupt absolutely," it does not see any solution in renouncing power. Instead, it asserts that only he who is willing to use power responsibly can challenge one who uses power irresponsibly. Because no sociopolitical action can be perfect, the Christian must be ready to "sin boldly," he must be prepared to make ambiguous choices among the live options. Politics is the art of the possible: the perfect way is never possible. By defending a lesser evil, we may hope to avert a greater evil.

There is much to justify this "orthodox" position. It is founded on a realistic and Christian view of man and his sin. It has proved highly congenial to social scientists and politicians. As a result, theologians have had the heady thrill of being listened to in affairs of state. But in the light of Barth and Bonhoeffer's analysis of sanctification, this is a reason to be suspicious of the position. It is strange that its Christian exponents have not had to swim against the stream but that, on the contrary, they have been lauded and praised. Many of the social scientists who have praised the position have affirmed that it is good politics, but they see nothing specifically Christian about it. From the point of view of the rediscovery of sanctification, this sounds as though the position may have capitulated to its social ethos.

This "orthodox" view of social ethics seemed particularly geared to America's situation in the cold war. However, in recent years there has been considerable heart searching, even in the secular world. Viet Nam and the Dominican Republic have caused many to wonder if pure political opportunism and cynicism have replaced all ethical concerns.[11] In such a wider debate, it will be interesting to see if the theological concern with sanctification will have a contribution to make.

The "orthodox" position held its place, in part, because much of its opposition came from those who held an obviously unrealistic view of human goodness. But the new doctrines of sanctification take as realistic a view of human nature as the prevailing "orthodoxy." These new doctrines affirm, however, that Christ has won a victory over the powers of this world, so that what is impossible with man is possible with God. What may this mean for social ethics? Charles West pointed out sometime ago that in the communist countries Barth was of greater practical help to the Christian than was Reinhold Niebuhr. Niebuhr's call to use power responsibly was of no value to those who had no power, or hope of getting power. Barth's theology, however, helped Christians in communist countries to remain responsibly Christian and to sing the Lord's song in a very strange land.[12] Perhaps in this age of thermonuclear warfare, when all use of power has become problematical, Barth may yet prove to have pointed the way. At any rate, it would seem that this will be an area of debate for some time.

The third feature in the rediscovery of sanctification is that it sees sanctification in an indispensable relationship to the church. Both classical liberalism and fundamentalism tended to ignore the church. Fundamentalism concentrated on the saving of individuals. Liberalism, at least in its social gospel wing, looked beyond individual salvation to the saving of society, but even so it seldom saw the church as anything more than another social organization. The classical liberal text, W. N. Clarke's *An Outline of Christian Theology,* has only one reference to the church in its index. The new concern with sanctification, however, both presupposes and extends the rediscovery of the church in modern theology.

Barth's doctrine of sanctification presupposes the church. No man becomes a Christian until another man mediates God's love to him. "What would I be if this other were not to me a witness of God, . . . of the divine work which affects me too, of my liberation for the love of God?"[13] And, Barth continues, the love of God would mean nothing to a man if he did not strive to share it with others. In short, Barth sees man's sanctification as being made possible only within the fellowship of those who know and witness to God's love.

Bonhoeffer's last chapter in *The Cost of Discipleship* gives particular emphasis to the place of the church in sanctifying the Christian. Here he advocates that the church has an obligation to discipline its members, an idea that still shocks most American Christians. In his book, *Life Together,* he draws out in more detail how the church can be the means whereby the Christian is aided in the living of the Christian life.

The New Testament scholar, Roy Harrisville, has made an important contribution at this point. He discusses the Christian concept of the new birth. Some, he points out, have described the new birth as simply a change in man's status before God. Whereas a man formerly stood under the wrath and condemnation of God, when he is "born again," he is forgiven and received by God. The new birth does not, however, result in any observable change in a man. God treats him "as if" he were righteous although, in fact, he is not. In opposition to the former view, the new birth often has been described simply in terms of a Christian's growth in observable piety. We know that a man is born again because he is diligent in prayer, church attendance, and probably because he gives up certain habits. Harrisville finds both viewpoints inadequate. The first sees clearly that the new birth depends upon God's act and not upon the believer's achievements, but it loses the Bible's emphasis upon discipleship and obedience. The second preserves the Biblical imperative that we follow Christ, but it fails to do justice to the obviously ambiguous nature of all believers' achievements. Who can point to consistent progress in his obedience to Christ? Both views fail, Harrisville believes, because "they have treated the rebirth in an exclusively individualistic fashion."[14]

Against these views, Harrisville argues that the New Testament never treats the new birth in terms of the believer as an isolated entity. Paul always sees man's life lived in a "field of being." He is "in Adam" or he is "in Christ." For Paul these are not abstractions; they are empirical realities. To be "in Adam" is to be identified with the society of unbelieving mankind. It is to express the spirit of one's age and social environment. To be "in Christ" is not a matter of an individualistic psychological experience of salvation; it is to be identified with the community that confesses Christ to be its Lord. Apart from the community of those who are the body of Christ, the church, there is no new birth, no sanctification.

The church also plays a crucial role in Emil Brunner's doctrine of sanctification. Brunner puts his treatment of sanctification within the context of his discussion of the Holy Spirit and the church.

Brunner finds a basic weakness in Bultmann's thought to be Bultmann's treatment of the activity of the Holy Spirit as a myth.[15] We can see the importance of the Holy Spirit, Brunner believes, only when we see that man is so entangled in his sin of egocentricity and pride that he resists any attack upon his autonomy. The doctrine of the Holy Spirit scandalizes sinful man because it tells him that he can be saved only by help from beyond himself. Is man's sin not so serious as Christians have believed? Can man save himself by his own efforts? The Christian answer is that the Holy Spirit comes to man to give him the power for a new life.

But, Brunner affirms, the Holy Spirit does not come to man in isolation. "All individualism as a religiosity directed to the salvation of one's own soul is a contradiction of the will of God revealed in Jesus Christ."[16] All too often Protestants have first dealt with the doctrine of faith and its relationship to the Holy Spirit, and then they have turned to a doctrine of the church as a sort of accidental aid to the life of faith. But this is to misunderstand both the life of faith and the church says Brunner. On the other hand, he does not believe that it is any better to turn to the Orthodox or Catholic position with its affirmation that there is no salvation outside of the church. The error in both Protestant and Catholic formulations is that they identify the church with an institution. This error in thought has become so pervasive, Brunner believes, that it is no longer meaningful to translate the New Testament word *ekklēsia* by our word "church." The Ekklesia is always a people. A people *has* institutions but it never itself *is* an institution. Thus where "church" means primarily an institution, we can no longer understand the New Testament.

In the New Testament, affirms Brunner, there is no salvation apart from the Ekklesia. But "the Ekklesia is never conceived of as institution; but exclusively as a fellowship of persons, as the common life based in fellowship with Jesus Christ as a fellowship of the Spirit (koinōnia pneumatos) and a fellowship of Christ (koinōnia Christou)."[17] Like Harrisville, Brunner affirms that to be "in Christ" is to be in this fellowship. The Ekklesia is thus the new humanity that God has willed in which persons live a common life based on fellowship with God and their brothers.

In earlier writings Brunner analyzed the essence of Christian faith in terms of a man's I-thou encounter with God in Christ. Now he shows how this person-to-person relationship of God and man occurs within the context of a fellowship of persons. As a fellowship of persons, the church is a redemptive community in which, and only in which, Christian sanctification can occur. When the church is thought of as an institution, the moral failures of the institution are so obvious that it is impossible to identify it with the holiness of the church, so theologians had to invent the concept of the invisibility of the true church. The Ekklesia is never invisible. It becomes visible, however, not as an institution but as a fellowship of persons who bear one another's burdens and aid one another in their growth in sanctification.

We might sum up the concern for the church among those who have rediscovered sanctification by saying that these theologians do not see the Christian as a "Lone Ranger" who rides off in lonely individualism to serve God and become righteous. Rather, they see the Christian as one who grows into his Christian life in continual relationship with others who, like him, are living in Christ's presence. Without the mutual guidance, witness, reproof, and even perhaps the discipline of one's fellow Christians, no individual could resist the pressures of the world that confront him "in Adam."

The new concern with sanctification in theology can be seen as an attempt to do justice to two basic New Testament themes. On the one hand, the New Testament emphasizes that man is a sinner who is helpless to do anything for himself. His only hope lies in the forgiving love of God. But this man, forgiven by God's love through Christ, has laid upon him the stern call to discipleship. On the one hand he is not saved by good works, but on the other hand, he *is* saved *for* good works, as Barth puts it. Because of the tension between these two themes, Christians have at times emphasized man's helplessness to the point where they have lost sight of the need of, or the hope for, a new life. At other times, the emphasis upon the new life has been such that its attainment has become a new law imposed upon man with the implication that he can fulfill it if he will but try. The new concern with sanctification is trying to do justice to both New Testament themes.

The concern for sanctification, as we have discussed it, transcends theological schools of thought. Those who are dedicated to it are not in complete agreement with one another. But the fact that men of differing theologies and backgrounds are converging on this doctrine indicates that it represents an area of vital concern to theology and the church today.

Chapter VI

Beyond Religion to Worldly Christianity

A major theme that runs through theology today speaks of "going beyond religion" to a "worldly" or "secular" Christianity. There is perhaps no aspect of theological jargon that causes more confusion among the laity than an appeal for worldly or religionless Christianity. Given the normal use of words, Christianity is a religion and to be Christian without being religious sounds like drawing a square without four sides. When a layman reads in his daily newspaper that a theologian has declared that "secularism is the will of God" he rubs his eyes; it sounds about the same as if the theologian had spoken a few words on behalf of the devil. Often the layman feels that he has been abandoned by theology in his battle to resist being conformed to the world. (Rom. 12:2.) In other cases the layman is overjoyed to learn that he can quit worrying about keeping himself unstained from the world. (James 1:27.) But in either case the layman is likely to be confused.

The clergyman too is confused. During the fifties of this century, while church membership was skyrocketing, the clergyman grew used to hearing theological leaders denounce this religious revival. He was told that religion was popular because the church had capitulated to the "world" in the form of "the American way of life." Church membership was just another worldly activity of the organization man. But, in the sixties, theology seems to have made a shift. Instead of denouncing the world's dominance of the church, it is calling the church to become worldly. The preacher who wants to be up-to-date theologically has to throw away his sermons of the fifties and come out with new ones praising secularism and berating the religious activities of the long-suffering laymen who come to hear him.

This confusion is found in the highest echelons of the church. Dean Peerman found it rampant among the delegates of the World Council of Churches Commission on World Missions and Evangelism that met in Mexico City early in 1964. With what Peerman describes as a "worldlier than thou" attitude, many of the delegates hailed the secularization of nations with rejoicing. Others protested that this "Hallelujah for secularism" hardly coincided with the cries of despair coming from the people of the most completely secularized nations.[1]

The distinction between Biblical faith and "religion" is by no means new. In the Old Testament we see the prophets engaged in a mortal battle with religious activities that took the form of idolatry. In the New Testament we see religious leaders providing the primary opposition to Jesus. As Reinhold Niebuhr warned us sometime ago, religion is not necessarily good; it may even be man's final stronghold against God. In the past, however, when theologians attacked religion, the hearer could expect a call to renounce false religion for the sake of pure or true religion. Frequently this call is not forthcoming from the critics of "religion" today.

If there is ambiguity in the word "religion," there is also ambiguity in the word "worldly." In the New Testament, the Greek words for "world" (*kosmos* and *aeon*) have double meanings. Sometimes they are used simply to describe the totality of creation, and, as such, the world is good. (Acts 17:24; Rom. 1:20.) On the other hand, they are used frequently to refer to mankind in its ignorance and rebellion against God, and as such the world is the chief enemy of Christ and the chief threat to the Christian. (Matt. 13:22; John 1:10; I Cor. 1:20.) So conceived, the world has fallen under the power of Satan. (I John 5:19.) It hates Christ and his disciples because they are not of the world. (John 7:7; 15:19.) Nonetheless, it is the "world" that God so loved that he gave his son to save it (John 3:16), and the world is the field into which the gospel is sent. (Matt. 13:38.)[2] It is evident that, if we are to do justice to the New Testament, we cannot be content with any simple acceptance or rejection of the "world."

To understand the concerns being expressed in terms such as "religionless" or "worldly" Christianity, we need to take a brief look at how the words came into modern theology. Behind the modern discussion lies primarily the work of Karl Barth. Barth made the distinction between Christian faith and religion so sharp that he could title one of the sections of his *Dogmatics* "The Revelation of God as the Abolition of Religion."[3] Barth defines religion as man's search for God and distinguishes it from revelation, which is God's search for man. In religion, man "finds" the god that he wants to find and thus his religion becomes a wall between him and God. In religion, including the Christian religion, man speaks, but in revelation God calls man to listen.

Christian religion is not less idolatrous than other religions, and the Christian does not dare to make any criticism of other religions that he does not first make of his own. Peter stands as the symbol of Christian religion and when the church affirms that Peter is the rock upon which it is founded, it would do well to take a close look at Peter. When Peter speaks by the inspiration of God he is the rock. (Matt. 16:17-18.) But when he speaks for himself, he is rebuked for savoring of the things of men. (Matt. 16:23.) The same is true for all the disciples. "So far as they stand on their own feet, the four Gospels make it quite clear that they are wholly and utterly outside. . . . They have their religion but it is equally clear that their religion is unbelief."[4] Nothing in the Christian religion justifies Christians in their missionary efforts. We cannot prove Christianity superior to other religions. Missionary activity is justified only when it points beyond man's religion to God's act in Christ.

But if man cannot save himself by his religion, Barth is equally sure that he cannot save himself by irreligion. Barth says there are two ways of attempting to overcome religion—mysticism and atheism. Mysticism sees the weakness of outward religious expressions, but it does not attack them. It retires to the inner life and reinterprets them. The mystic is still seeking his own salvation through his own efforts. The atheist, at first sight, seems to have gone beyond religion, for he renounces all its forms. But, in fact, he is not so deeply critical as the mystic. He scores a few points against some obvious weaknesses of religion, but he accepts "with the happiest and most naive credulity" the authorities of nature, history, civilization and rational existence, and some ethic. Atheism's attempt to overcome religion provides opportunity for the rise of new religions.[5]

Barth does not advocate a "religionless Christianity." He sees the situation as similar to that of the law. Man, in his sin, tries to save himself by doing the works of the law. However, when man receives his justification by faith from God he does not live an antinomian life, he fulfills the spirit of the law. Similarly, sinful man tries to save himself through his religious activity, but the justified man does not become irreligious. The Christian knows that no religion, including the Christian religion, can make itself true. But the Christian has faith that, as the sinner is justified, so God's grace may redeem sinful religion. "Revelation can adopt religion and mark it off as true religion."[6]

Barth forces Christians to look upon their religious life with a radical humility. The dichotomies that they make between religion and the world, or the sacred and the profane, are called into question. Religion, as man's idolatrous flight from God, is found on both sides of all such dichotomies. Barth helps us to see why the prophets and Jesus found their chief opponents among the religious people.

Barth's distinction between faith and religion leads to a rejection of the common division between religious and secular life. The Bible, he tells us, has no idea of a "special religious activity." Christians are not called to a few particular "religious" actions; they are called to serve God "in the whole range of their humanity."[7] The salvation of the individual Christian is not the final meaning of God's grace or the final aim of Christian life. The Christian is called to love God's world even in its fallen state. The Christian must serve God in the secular sphere, in economics and politics, as well as the academic and aesthetic realms.[8]

Barth's distinction between faith and religion and his emphasis upon the calling of the Christian to serve God in the world anticipates many of the features of the contemporary theological concern with worldly Christianity. But the main currents of this theological concern have not come directly from Barth; they have been inspired by Dietrich Bonhoeffer. Bonhoeffer's comments on worldly Christianity are both suggestive and tantalizing. The most vivid comments are found in his letters written from prison shortly before his martyrdom under the Nazis. There is still a lively debate about who the "real" Bonhoeffer is and how these letters are to be related to his earlier works. Because the statements in the letters are suggestive rather than systematic, they have inspired a variety of interpretations.

Bonhoeffer's points, which have stirred contemporary theology, begin with his assertion that the world "has come of age," it is in its adulthood, men have grown beyond religion.[9] They no longer try to explain the gaps in their knowledge by referring piously to God. In both their theoretical and their practical lives, men find that they can get along very well without God. In the past, religion has claimed the "ultimate" questions for itself, but today man is handling these ultimate questions without even referring to religion.

Throughout its history, Christianity has presupposed that man is, by nature, religious. One of its favorite forms of apologetics has been to claim that Christianity is the true religion, in which men may find what they have been seeking in other religions. But what happens if, as Bonhoeffer believes, man has outgrown religion? Has the time come when, if a man is to become a Christian, he must come without first being religious?

How do we win men for Christ in an age that has matured beyond religion? Bonhoeffer did not have time to work out his answer. He did foresee some difficulties. A

new language for faith had to be found but he confessed
that the job of finding a nonreligious interpretation of the
Bible proved more difficult than he had anticipated.[10] He
was sure that a nonreligious interpretation would seek to
find God in man's strength and knowledge, and not in the
gaps where man was weak and ignorant. He poured con-
tempt upon attempts to commend God by first proving to
men that they are miserable even though they think that
they are happy. When psychotherapists and existentialist
philosophers tried likewise to gain their ends by driving
men to despair, Bonhoeffer called their efforts "secularized
methodism."[11] Such spiritual blackmail deserved to fail,
and it would fail.

Bonhoeffer argued that the Christian life is not a salvation from the world. Instead, the Christian must live a
"worldly" life; he must not strive to be a saint, he must
strive to be a man. "Jesus does not call men to a new
religion, but to life."[12] The Christian believes in the Jesus
Christ who took the worldly paths of weakness and suffer-
ing. Likewise, the Christian must take this life in his
stride, entering into the ways of the world to serve God.

It is evident that in his radical distinction between religion and Christian faith, Bonhoeffer is walking in Barth's
footsteps. But there are important differences. The most
obvious is Bonhoeffer's claim that man has moved beyond
religion, while Barth argues that man, even in atheism, is
religious. Barth argues that revelation can create true religion as Grace creates a new man, while Bonhoeffer insists
that Christianity must transcend religion. And yet, before
deciding that these are absolute differences, we must ask if
both men mean the same thing by religion.

For Barth, religion is man's striving to make himself
righteous before that which he recognizes as ultimate and

decisive. Even the atheist does not escape religion in this sense. He destroys the old gods only to capitulate to "other dogmas of truth and ways of certainty, which may at any moment take on a religious character."[13]

Bonhoeffer does not offer a definition of religion in his letters, but we get a fairly precise idea of what he means. When the man on the street speaks of religion, he thinks of churches, worship, prayer, and associated activities. Bonhoeffer certainly does not mean to cast all of this aside, for he asks, "What is the place of worship and prayer in the entire absence of religion?"[14] Furthermore, the non-religious language for which he searches can come, he tells us, only through prayer and doing right by our fellowmen.[15]

When Bonhoeffer speaks of the end of religion, he seems to have in mind three things. First, he sees the end of the traditional distinction between the sacred and the secular realms, with "religion" confined to the former. The essence of Bonhoeffer's position is his concern to affirm with Luther that Christian faith is not a matter for the sacred sphere of the monastery and religious "good works," but faith sends us to serve God in daily toil at the office, the kitchen, or the factory. Secondly, by religion, Bonhoeffer has in mind the concern for personal salvation with its corresponding works of piety to develop the "inner life" of the believer. Against such religion, Christianity calls us to serve the world in which we find ourselves, caring not first for our own salvation but for the welfare of our neighbor. Thirdly, by religion, Bonhoeffer means a metaphysical interpretation of the universe with God brought in to fill the gaps in our knowledge and with God waiting in the wings to come to our help when our own resources run out.

It is evident that Barth and Bonhoeffer are not far apart in their discussion of religion. If Bonhoeffer were using the word "religion" as Barth does, he would have to see Nazism as a demonic expression of religion with its worship of the gods of race and soil. In Barth's sense of the word, Bonhoeffer would not have said that man had grown beyond religion.

The mention of Nazism raises a serious problem for those who take up Bonhoeffer's statement about a world come of age. In English, at least, "come of age" has a connotation of maturity; it is a complimentary term. But if Nazism represents a world come of age, we might well seek a way back to childhood. It would seem that Bonhoeffer did not intend the phrase to carry any connotation of praiseworthiness. The German phrase that he used describes one who, having arrived at a certain age, is now on his own. He may use his independence for devilish purposes, but he cannot be restricted by returning him to the nursery.

Bonhoeffer's concepts have meant different things to different people. There have always been those who longed for a Christian faith that was not tied to churches, theology, clergy, or "organized religion" in general. Naturally these persons have hailed the slogans of a religionless Christianity in our time. Others find in the slogans little more than a new expression of the traditional Christian concern to apply the faith to the daily tasks of life. Today we do not have a Bonhoeffer school of theology; we have several different trends of thought inspired by him. We shall take a brief look at some of these.

The most common use of the slogan of a worldly Christianity is to emphasize the need to apply the Christian faith to the needs and problems of contemporary society. If Christ is truly Lord of the world, it is not enough to save a few souls from out of the world. Christ must be made real in and through the structures of society. It is not enough for the Christian to dedicate his energies to the business of organized religion and to be a faithful worker in his job. Christian faith must go forth to meet the challenges, needs, and evils in society. The Christian must march in civil rights demonstrations, register voters, take part in political parties, and join with men of goodwill who are fighting the forces of corruption wherever they are found.

So described, there does not seem to be anything radically new about worldly Christianity. We can find parallels to this in the church throughout its history. The Protestant Reformation called men out of the monasteries and sent them into the world. But even medieval Catholicism, despite its emphasis upon the monastery, had an abiding concern to structure the whole life of man under the Lordship of Christ. Protestantism, from Luther and Calvin to Rauschenbusch and Niebuhr, called Christians to responsible action in society.

Perhaps what is new about the present concern with worldly Christianity is expressed by Daniel Jenkins. He points out that in a sense this is simply the old call for Christians to live in the world and to overcome its destructive powers, but he says that its originality lies in its recognition of how "subtle and many sided" are the ways in which religion has been able to escape from its commitment to the world. Also, it is original in its "understanding of how complete an identification with the world in its need, and how great a power to overcome the world at its strongest, is possible for the man of faith."[10]

It was not too long ago that seminary graduates were going forth filled with the latest psychoanalytical theories and seeing themselves as spiritual counsellors to neurotic individuals. Theologically, they saw their goal as a creating of I-thou relationships to combat the loneliness and isolation of persons in our culture. Surely these concerns to meet the psychological and personal needs of individuals were legitimate tasks for the church. But, like other good things, they were often overemphasized. Peace of mind and togetherness cults were formed; the minister became an amateur psychiatrist and the couch replaced the altar as the sacramental center of the church. In part, the present concern with worldly Christianity is a reaction against these overemphases. Today the seminary graduate asks what is the use of curing individual neuroses, and then turning the cured ones loose in a sick world. Today's seminary graduate does not want to retire to his study to counsel with individuals; he feels called to march in civil rights demonstrations or to work for urban renewal.

In part, this concern with worldly Christianity is an extension of the concern with sanctification which we examined in the last chapter. Far too often in the past, the doctrine of sanctification has been concerned with the attainment of personal purity. But when sanctification was rediscovered by men like Bonhoeffer and Barth, it was placed in a context of concern for the total life of the world. Sanctification cannot be limited to a man's personal and family habits; it must also include how he votes and how he acts in the social struggles of his day.

Another feature of contemporary worldly Christianity is its determination to understand and serve the world as it is today. This is expressed most forcefully in Harvey Cox's *The Secular City*. His central theme is that today we live in a qualitatively different age from that of the past. Urbanization has brought a new way of life. Increased mobility has resulted in anonymity, impersonality, and the break up of long-term acquaintances. This results in tolerance of ethical differences. Men are forced to seek new methods for planning and rationally controlling human life. He calls this age "technopolis" and contrasts it to the former social forms of the "tribe" and "town." The tribal and town mentalities still live today, however, and there is an unfortunate tendency in the church to extol the values, ethical and otherwise, of these past eras. Cox's book is a sustained appeal to the Christian to accept the age in which he lives and to apply his faith to it, without getting lost in nostalgic memories of the "good old days."

Cox attempts to describe the age of technopolis or the "secular city" in an objective fashion. He tells us that "secularization is not the Messiah. But neither is it the anti-Christ."[17] However, he obviously looks upon the development of technopolis with considerable relish. It is a time of danger, he admits, but it is also a time of new freedoms and opportunities. He wants to see the church have its vital place in this new era. Instead of being a static institution, he calls the church to be God's *avant-garde* in the world. He quotes with approval Archie Hargrave's analogy of God's work as a "floating crap game" and the church as "a confirmed gambler" which arises each day anxious to know "where the action is."[18]

 There is another concern presented under the slogan of worldly Christianity. It is a protest that the church has become so involved with itself as an institution that it has lost its sense of mission and service to the world. In a rapidly changing world, the church moves on with the same kind of activities and organizations that it always had, even though these may no longer serve a real need in the world. Worse still, the dedicated layman is pressured to spend his time and energies in these activities so that he has little time for Christian witness or service in the various organizations of his community. The result is that church activity seems to many to have less and less to do with the concerns of everyday living.

Recently, my teen-age son's church youth group drew up a program. The topic for discussion was announced as "Does the church inspire youth today? Why not?" The topic expresses eloquently the conviction of many young people that there can be only a negative answer to the first question. Churchmen have become more and more self-critical of what the church is doing to preserve itself as an institution. They fear that Pierre Berton may be right when he charges that we have made the criterion of Christianity a matter of how often a man attends the "religious club."[19] Discussion of worldly Christianity thus becomes a way of asking how the church can truly be the church in the modern world.

One of the most powerful expressions of this concern is Colin Williams' *Where in the World*. He begins with the crisis of the parish, noting that there is a drop off in the number of candidates for the ministry, and that within seminaries a smaller percentage of students plan to go into the parish ministry. Many pastors of local congregations feel that the present structure of the church does not allow them to do their true work. Williams raises the question of whether the local congregation, with an ordained pastor and church building, is an adequate form for an age in which people no longer live where they work, and when the population is as mobile as it is today. In the past, church forms have altered with changing conditions, and they must do so today. But our problem is that "the local residence congregation is so turned inward that it is often well-nigh impossible to reverse its direction in order that its life may flow outward into the structure of the world's need."[20]

Another concern that is often expressed in the discussion of secular or worldly Christianity deals with the problem of language. It is pointed out that we live in an age for which traditional language about God is no longer meaningful. Men in our age have come to think of themselves as living in a one-story universe. They have no sense of the mystery or wonder of life. When someone speaks of God, the word does not refer to anything that modern man sees in his life. There are several reasons for this attitude, but many churchmen have come to the uncomfortable feeling that the language of Christian piety has helped to make God seem unreal. As Samuel Miller puts it, "We had effectively done away with Him; somewhere, we do not know quite where, we, the worshippers of God, the Christians, had buried Him."[21] Christians thus face the task of finding some way to express the reality of God in this age. How is the church to speak to this "secular city" in which it lives today?

For some years, theologians have referred to our age as one in which God seems to be silent, or absent. A few have used Nietzsche's radical phrase that "God is dead." To most theologians the phrase "God is dead" is a way of saying that modern man finds it difficult to see the reality of God. The theologian who does believe in God is thus concerned to see how he can speak to an age for whom God seems dead. But in recent years a small group of theologians have carried the theme of worldly Christianity farther still. They are not content to say that God *seems* dead to modern man; they claim that God *is* dead.

The exponents of the "God is dead" theology are not saying that we need a new concept of God. There always have been theologians who have declared, "Your concept of God is too small," and have thus implied the nonexistence of the god about whom the erroneous idea was held. But such theologians have called us to a higher and truer understanding of God. The "God is dead" theologians, however, have no higher concept of God; they tell us that we must get along without God.

William Hamilton says that there are two schools of Protestant religionlessness. For one, religion means "religious activities" such as liturgy, counseling, saying prayers, and going to church. The appeal for religionless Christianity is an appeal to reevaluate such activities and our past ways of doing them. Such considerations, he says, are popular in "denomination headquarters." But Hamilton wishes to defend a different form of "religionlessness." He defines religion as "any system of thought or action in which God or the gods serve as fulfiller of needs or solver of problems."[22] For Hamilton, to be religionless is to see that man has no need of God to help solve any problem or to save men from despair. It is to deny that man needs God or that there are any things which only God is qualified to do. Religionless Christianity means that man, come of age, is prepared to meet and handle his own problems without divine assistance.

From this brief summary of some of the themes involved in "worldly" Christianity, it is evident that the term does not cover any one school or train of thought. Jenkins is probably right in saying that terms such as "religionless Christianity" or "worldly Christianity" are not accurate descriptions of the concerns.[23] We saw that "the world" is used in different senses in the New Testament, and today it is probably even more loose in its meaning. In one sense of the word, the very thing that many of the exponents of the worldly Christianity are fighting is the "worldly" nature of the church. That is, the church has become too closely conformed to the mores and values of its culture to speak a word of judgment upon them. When an experiment was made a few months ago with radio commercials to "sell" Christian faith, it was, in one sense, a totally worldly expression of Christianity. But the exponents of a worldly Christianity were the ones who protested most loudly against this "worldly" experiment.

The same problem haunts the use of the word "secular." It can and does mean different things to different persons. To many persons secularism means simply life without God. As such, only the "God is dead" theologians could logically support a secular Christianity or applaud the growth of secularism. To others, secularism means freedom from ecclesiastical control and, as such, secularism may often be the will of God.

Harvey Cox makes a useful distinction between secularization and secularism. Secularization is the historical process in which "society and culture are delivered from tutelage to religious control and closed metaphysical world views." As such it is a liberating movement. But secularism is an ideology, a new, closed-world view that functions like a religion by making its interpretation of reality ultimate and something to be forced on everyone.[24] Secularization is really founded on the Bible, says Cox. Biblical revelation freed man from his belief that nature and society around him were sacred and awesome. Biblical secularization means that man does not need to bow before the forces of nature or society; he needs to bow only before the transcendent God. This frees man to use nature and reform society. Secularism, on the other hand, is a reversal of the Biblical thrust. It would restore the myths of sacredness to nature and to society and it would enslave men to particular ways of life.

Even when all the necessary distinctions have been made in the meaning of terms such as "worldly" and "secular," one still must wonder if their use in this context is not dangerous. According to the New Testament, the Christian is to serve the world because it is the world that God loves. He is not to become conformed to it, for if he does, he can no longer really be of service to it. The fact that God had to act to save the world indicates that he who would serve it most truly must not be conformed to it too closely. Can we still express this warning if we adopt too uncritically the language of worldly Christianity?

Langdon Gilkey has written one of the best-balanced books in this area. Its title expresses the problem, *How the Church Can Minister to the World Without Losing Itself*. Speaking from a deep historical knowledge, Gilkey does not assume that the contemporary search for relevance in the world is unique or new. He says that "all through the centuries the church has in one way or another been conscious that, like its Lord, his teachings, and its own hopes, it is *in* but not *of* the world. . . . The church, then, if it is to be itself and do its work, must mediate to the world some Word, some Presence, some norm and standard, that are both transcendent in their origin—in some measure 'holy'—and also relevant to the world's life."[25]

Gilkey does not take second place to any of the evangelists of worldly Christianity in his criticism of the existing church, but he does recognize that a basic problem in the church today is its "worldliness." The church has failed to disturb its culture with a prophetic word of judgment or of healing, because the church itself has become an expression of its culture. Thus, it is apparent that slogans like "worldly Christianity" are in danger of being too ambiguous. It is easy to justify one's complacent acceptance of the *status quo* by announcing that one is practicing worldly Christianity.

The church, says Gilkey, must somehow express holiness and transcendence in a way that is relevant to the life of the world. By holiness or transcendence he means that which comes from beyond any particular culture to judge and to heal it. Gilkey makes an important point because, without some such insight, the exponents of worldly Christianity are in danger of sounding like the newspapers' Sunday supplements with their continual hymns of praise to love, brotherhood, and tolerance. To put Jesus into this setting as the "man for others" is all too likely to make him just another ideal or example. Everyone applauds him in theory, but fails to follow him in practice. When Gilkey speaks of the need for the Holy and the transcendent, he reminds us that the world needs a savior, not an example.

There is a danger that the terminology of worldly Christianity may lead to an uncritical acceptance of all that the world has to offer. There is also a related danger that it may lead to an underevaluation of the sources of strength within the church. We must agree with the exponents of worldly Christianity who say that the Christian is called to spend time and energy in the structures of the secular world. As Gilkey points out, if all that a man can point to as evidence of his churchmanship is that he gives time, energy, and money to the activities of the church, he is speaking like a medieval believer in "good works." But we have no reason to suppose that the world would be better served if we closed down all church activities.

The Christian who goes into the world can serve it only if he has something to bring to it. In Gilkey's terms, he must know the Holy and the transcendent. But from whence can he gain this except through the life of the church, where the Word is heard and the Sacraments are received. We are told that it was the custom of Jesus to go to the synagogue on the Sabbath day. (Luke 4:16.) Jesus was not one to follow a custom for custom's sake. Jesus was, as the worldly Christians tell us, "a Man for others," but he was also one who recognized that he needed both times of corporate worship and private prayer if he was to be truly for others. Bonhoeffer rightly warned us that we ought not to be more religious than God; we also need to be warned not to try to be more worldly than Jesus.

But the problem goes even deeper. A significant part of the world is the congregation. In some ways those who preach worldly Christianity do not seem to have outgrown the sacred-secular dichotomy that they deplore. Thus they draw their own line between the church and the world and imply that time spent in the church is time deprived from the world. But anyone who knows an average congregation knows that the world marches into church every Sunday morning. Some of these worldlings in the church know and have accepted Christ's Lordship but many of them seem scarcely to know of it and certainly they have not accepted it. Within the life of this congregation are many ways, some still untapped, in which to serve the "world."

The church has a mission to unite and reconcile all men in Christ. Men are divided by barriers of race, class, culture, nation, and religion. Colin Williams speaks for many when he affirms that the residential congregation cannot perform this mission. He says: "Is it not true that in our world in varying degrees men do come together across these barriers in other activities of life—at work, in politics, in health, in mass entertainments—but that church life is related to men at the place of their greatest separation (residence), and takes on very little form at the places where the world gives an opportunity to break through these separations?"[26] One does not have to pretend that the local church is fulfilling its mission or that its work does not need to be supplemented to argue that such a statement overlooks some important features.

In the first place, Williams' statement gives an overly optimistic picture of the worlds of work and play. In fact, most persons find that their work is a highly segregated part of life. Quite frequently it is racially and sexually segregated, always it is segregated by social, educational, and economic lines. In entertainment, there is a rigid economic segregation, for example the barrier between those who can and those who cannot afford a private country club. Even public golf courses draw different classes of people depending upon the amount of their daily fees.

On the other hand, Williams' reference to the "residence" congregation sounds as though today's congregation had not changed from the days when all parishioners lived within hearing distance of the bell in the steeple. As a matter of fact, it is quite common for churchmen to drive considerable distances to their place of worship. When they get there they find that they are worshiping with persons who do not live in their area at all. Congregational activities bring together persons of widely different economic, educational, cultural, and ethnic backgrounds. Corporation lawyers, industrialists, and professors work with garage mechanics, chauffeurs, and carpenters. Furthermore, these congregational contacts lead to friendships and social mixing outside the congregational activities. In fact, the congregational life does not exist separate from the world, but the world comes to it and goes out from it with new relationships.

One of the serious failures of most congregations is that they have done little to break down racial barriers. But even here failure is not the whole story. The racial problem must be solved on many levels. At present the civil rights campaigns have put the legal questions of justice at the center. The battle to win simple justice for the Negro and other minorities has been a long and difficult one and the end is not yet here. But even when the legal battle for justice is won, as it will be, the white man and the Negro may work together in mutual distrust, suspicion, and prejudice. Where, however, a local parish has accepted members of another race, there is a unique opportunity for fellow members of a worshiping congregation to get to know one another as persons and to cross the barriers.

All of this is not to pretend that the local congregation is fulfilling its calling or that it should be made immune from criticism. But it is to remind us that, amid all the concern with worldly and religionless Christianity, we ought not to forget that important and potentially significant part of the world that we call the local congregation. When all the criticism has been heaped on the local congregation, we still have the ironical fact that most of its theological critics came to the Christian faith through local congregations. The critics are employed by institutions that depend primarily on local congregations for their support. The critics' books are bought and read primarily by parish ministers and members of their little flocks. The local congregation seems likely to be the foundation for any new forms of the church that may appear.

Religionless Christianity is an important and authentic note in the life of the church today. Although, as Gilkey sees, it is a problem about which the church has always agonized, it is one that comes with its unique features in our times. If in our last pages we have made some reservations, it is not because we would question the central concerns of the movement. We do question the wisdom of some of its terminology and some of its more enthusiastic utterances. If we are critical of these, it is not because we doubt the importance of the concerns. Rather, we consider these so important that we do not want to see them identified with a theological fad so that they are dropped when the fad passes from the center of the stage.

Chapter VII

Theology in Dialogue

An often amusing but nonetheless effective method of locating the vital theological issues in any age is to look for the "sacred" words that most often occur where theologians gather. At various times in the last two decades, this method would have located central issues by noting the use of "confrontation," "I and thou," *agapē* and *erōs*, and "demythologization." Today it is obvious that the most sacred theological word is "dialogue."

We hear a great deal about the dialogue between Roman Catholicism and Protestantism. Pope Paul VI has also stressed the need for dialogue with the world, and a striking fruit of this concern has been the holding of meetings between European Catholic and Communist leaders. A recently founded Protestant journal bears the name *Dialog*. Theologians everywhere are making efforts to enter into dialogue with the sciences, the arts, and the world about them. There has been so much emphasis upon dialogue that some punster has warned that we are in danger of replacing a theology of the Word by wordiness.

What lies behind this widespread concern with dialogue? One obvious answer is that theology has become more humble. There was a time when theology did not deign to converse with the secular arts and sciences. Instead, theology moved imperiously in their midst as the "Queen of the Sciences." A queen does not hold dialogues with her subjects; at best she grants an audience. Theology, as queen, was prepared to tell the arts and sciences what they could or could not do and what their legitimate places were. Theology, as queen, assumed that she held a vantage point above the other sciences so that she knew the real meaning of each of the sciences better than they could know it themselves. But a theology that is prepared to enter into dialogue with these disciplines is thereby admitting the equality of its partners in the dialogue.

Modern theologians are vividly aware of the finite and human nature of their efforts. One reason that Roman Catholic and Protestant can enter into dialogue today is that on both sides, it is recognized that theology is not an infallible science. Roman Catholics have pointed out that although their church is founded on dogmas of the faith that are believed to be infallible, this infallibility does not rub off onto the work of those who interpret dogma. In the same way the new conservative Protestant believes in an inerrant Bible, but he does not claim inerrancy for his interpretation of it. Karl Barth is widely hailed as the man who brought about the great revival of theology in our time, but from the beginning he insisted that every theology is a finite effort that must continually be judged by the revealed Word. Furthermore, he emphasized that no theology can be final; it can only be a more or less adequate expression of the faith for the time in which it appears. Far from being a ruling queen, such theology is hardly even a constitutional monarch.

When theology grows humble, it knows that it needs to learn from the world. No longer does the theologian have a metaphysical map marked with the preordained place for each of the sciences. The theologian must listen to the science in question so that he may learn what is its place. Theology also needs to learn from the world because, as we saw in the last chapter, it has a revived concern to serve the world. To be helpful, therefore, it must first listen and let the world express its needs.

The period in which theology has grown humble is also a period in which there has been a growing conviction that theology is an inescapable vocation in the life of every Christian. The Christian who claims to have no theology is, in fact, hiding from himself the theological premises by which he lives and as a result he fails to bring them under any creative criticism. As theology has grown humble, there has been a new breakthrough in theology for the laity. We have discovered the theologianhood of all believers. Because theology is no longer seen as the monopoly of a few experts, the experts recognize their need to enter into dialogue with other Christians if a theology of the whole church is to be developed.

Dialogue also is a sacred word today because the church is filled with a sense of the urgency of its speaking to the unbelieving world. To understand the significance of this phenomenon, we need to look at another of the sacred words in theology today—relevance. Wherever Christians gather, they seem to get a masochistic glee out of analyzing how irrelevant they are to the world in which they find themselves. Dialogue with the world is thus sought in hope of finding why the church seems irrelevant and to learn how it may become relevant.

This concern with relevance occurs in a period of almost unbelievable change and development in the world. Science and learning are progressing at such a rapid speed that in many disciplines those who graduated ten years ago are now in need of returning to school if they are not to be completely out of date. Technological change is re-

molding man's life in every area so that the urgent problems of yesterday are gone—but scores of new problems
have arisen! In a period of such change, we can no longer
sing with comfort the words of the old hymn, "Thy church
. . . a thousand years the same." Can an unchanging church
be relevant in a changing world like ours?

At first sight, it might seem that the anxiety over relevance is a neurotic attitude in the church today. True, the
European churches are not numerically large but they are
certainly no worse off today than they have been for most
of the last century. In America, the churches had their
greatest upsurge in membership during the fifties, and although their phenomenal growth has tapered off, they are
holding their own statistically. For an "irrelevant" group,
the churches seem to interest a lot of people.

Despite the many signs of health, however, a number of
observers have detected warning signs. Large sections of
society, including college students and organized labor,
are seriously alienated from the church. Although the population has shifted drastically from a rural to an urban
one, the American churches are still fumbling in their
attempts to find their place in the city.

Pierre Berton points out that "the twentieth century
marks the first time in the church's long history that it
has lost control of *all* the contemporary means of communication." In the Middle Ages the church had a monopoly on education; until Shakespeare's time it controlled
the theater; for many years it controlled painting and
sculpture and music. But today the forces that are molding
public opinion are outside of the church's influence and
are often in the hands of those who are indifferent to, or
alienated from, the Christian faith.[1]

Still another disturbing sign is the evidence that membership in a church is frequently unrelated to any accep-

tance of Christianity as a way of life. It is argued that despite its growth in membership, the contemporary American church has less influence on the wider life of the nation than ever before in its history. This was illustrated dramatically in California during the 1964 election. A plebiscite was held on "Proposition 14" to make antidiscriminatory housing laws unconstitutional. California church leaders, in amazing numbers, rose up to work for the defeat of the proposition. Despite the fact, however, that the majority of Californians are members of churches, the proposition carried by a 2-1 margin. This is seen as evidence that many who join the church do not find Christian faith relevant to the important decisions that they have to make in the world.

Behind the loss of intellectuals and the failure of the church to inspire its members to Christian action, many see a failure of Christian language. The church speaks a tongue that no longer communicates. Thus secular authors, whose interests are close to those of Christian theology, often fail to see through the theological language to the common concerns. Even church members have failed to see any connection between the pious language they hear on Sunday and the practical affairs they face the rest of the week.

If its language seems irrelevant, the church must enter into dialogue with the world; it must listen to the world and learn, so that it can speak relevantly to it. A pioneer in dialogue was Paul Tillich. At the very center of his theology, he put his method of correlation. Theology must operate, he said, by correlating its answers to the questions that man actually asks.[2] We can almost say that, for Tillich, theology does not *enter* into dialogue with the world, it *is* dialogue with the world. Similarly, Rudolf Bultmann's program of demythologization can be seen as an effort at dialogue. The strange language of Biblical myth is to be interpreted through the thought forms of modern man as found in Heidegger's existential analysis.

From the beginning, the ways of dialogue raised questions. To be relevant to modern man, Tillich spoke of God as "the Ground of Being." Perhaps this is relevant, for even the atheist must confess that there is some ground to his being. But, in attempting to be relevant, has theology been cut loose from its moorings in historical Christianity? Can we identify the Ground of Being with the God and Father of Jesus Christ? When I was dealing with Tillich in one of my courses, a student came to class early and wrote on the blackboard, "The ground of being is dirt." His semifacetious remark found serious support as both philosophers and theologians discussed whether Tillich was an atheist. In our discussion of the demythologization debate, we saw that many critics charge that Bultmann has lost much of the essence of Christian faith. Furthermore, we found that some of his left-wing followers have advocated an abandonment of the kerygma itself. As we look back, it appears that, whether they succeeded or not, it was the intention of both Tillich and Bultmann to preserve and make relevant the essentials of Christian faith. Today, however, there are many theologians who openly abandon this intention.

When we examine the contemporary concern with dialogue, we find two major trends that threaten to split theology more decisively than any of the former theological debates of this century. Both trends recognize the need for dialogue with the world and both are attempting to engage in it. One trend, however, is working on the assumption that the changes in the modern world have resulted in a qualitative transformation of man and his thinking. As a result, theologians in this trend believe that modern man can accept the Christian message only if it is changed drastically. The second trend includes theologians who admit that we live in a fast-changing world and that we must strive to translate the faith for modern men. But they do not agree that the essentials of the faith must be changed or abandoned.

Because the distinction between these trends has only recently begun to come to light, and because those within each of the trends do not agree completely with each other, we do not have any established terms with which to describe the trends. The first trend is widely referred to as "radical" or "left wing" theology. Presumably this makes the second trend conservative or middle-of-the-road. But this is not a useful terminology. From the point of view of traditional Christian faith, the first trend is radical, while the second is more conservative. But, from the point of view of the main currents of thought today, it is the first group that identifies itself with the *status quo,* and it is the second group that brings a radical criticism of the modern world. For the sake of convenience, we shall refer to those who follow the first trend as "transformers," and to those who follow the second trend as "translators." Although many in the first trend speak of what they are doing as "translating," and many in the second speak of themselves as "transforming" the message of the church, our usage of the terms has some merit. To transform something normally implies a drastic change. A translation, however, implies that although we are speaking in a different language, we are still saying the same thing.

The battle lines between these two groups are not yet hard and fast. There are a number of men who are on the border lines and might be put into either camp. For example, in his *Honest to God*, Bishop Robinson sounded like a transformer. He said that he could understand those who urge that we should give up speaking of God for a generation.[3] Statements about God, he affirmed, are really statements about the "ultimacy" of personal relationships.[4] He called for a new morality[5] and a new way to pray.[6] But in his more recent book, *The New Reformation?* Robinson sounds like a translator. He denies that he wishes to reduce Christianity to humanism.[7] He affirms that even "after his death" God "is disturbingly alive."[8] To clarify the nature of the two groups we shall choose representatives who clearly represent the division.

The "God is dead" theologians represent the transformers. It hardly needs to be argued that if we present the Christian faith without God, we have transformed the nature of its message. Thomas Altizer has expressed the point clearly. The "contemporary theologian," he tells us, "knows that he is not a Christian in any sense that could be drawn from the creeds and confessions of the historic church."[9] For the God is dead theology, a change has come over the world, so that it is no longer possible to believe in God. As William Hamilton says: "And this is an experience that is not peculiar to a neurotic few, nor is it private or inward. Death of God is a public event in our history, we are saying."[10]

Van Buren claims that modern "secular" man cannot understand language about God. Thus, when Bonhoeffer or Ebeling seek to speak of God in a "worldly" way, he charges that they are evading the real problem because they are still trying to speak about God, and that is what modern man cannot understand. "The empiricist in us finds the heart of the difficulty not in what is said about

God, but in the very talking about God at all. We do not know 'what' God is, and we cannot understand how the word 'God' is being used."[11]

If God is dead, what is left that is Christian? The "God is dead" theologians believe that modern man can have loyalty to the man, Jesus, and they claim that their commitment to Jesus means that they are still within the Christian framework. Of course, the Jesus that modern man can accept is not the unique son of God or the risen Lord. He was a man like us in all ways except that he was "a man for others," one who lived in service to his fellowmen. As such, Jesus retains his power to win men.

As Christians we do not look for a god to come to our aid, but we do seek to find Jesus where he may be found today. Hamilton says: "Jesus may be concealed in the world, in the neighbor, in this struggle for justice, in that struggle for beauty, clarity, order. Jesus is in the world as masked and the work of the Christian is to strip off the masks of the world to find him."[12] If a critic says that such a theology has become no more than ethics, van Buren has a ready answer. "In a secular age, what would that 'more' be?"[13] He affirms that alchemy was "reduced" to chemistry and astrology to astronomy. In the same way he believes that the time has come to "reduce" theology to ethics. Theology, freed of its metaphysical bondage, can turn its attention to the human, the historical, and the empirical.

The "God is dead" theology tries to distinguish itself from more familiar forms of atheism and thus justify its claim to be theological and Christian. Altizer has continued to speak of the "sacred," although he cannot speak of God. Often using mystical language, he encourages us to find the sacred in and through the profane. Van Buren attempts to show that his secular meaning of the gospel gets to the heart of what the Bible and the historic creeds were really trying to say. Hamilton at one time said that the "God is dead" theologian is still waiting for God, although, in personal conversation, he has indicated that he no longer holds this position.

The real heart of the "God is dead" theology, however, seems to be a call to accept the modern world and all that it means. Altizer tells us that "a theologian who cannot affirm his own destiny—the actual moment of time in which he exists—has ceased to be Christian."[14] As a result, "we know that Christ is present in the concrete actuality of our history or he is not truly present at all." Van Buren is ready to concede that secularism is neither a better nor a worse mode of thought than that of ancient times. But, with an almost fatalistic attitude, he goes on to affirm that it is the only way of thought man can understand today.[15]

Hamilton describes this acceptance of the modern world in terms of Luther's movement from the cloister to the world. Furthermore, he does not mean what so many theologians mean when they speak of going to the world. They speak of going to pessimistic writers like Kafka or Beckett to get illustrations for their doctrines of sin. But Hamilton, in a startling passage, affirms that he does not go to the world of these "modern" writers, he goes into the world they reject—"the world of technology, power, money, sex, culture, race, poverty, and the city."[16] Hamilton's position is based upon an optimism about man and his abilities. In developments like the civil rights movement, man is standing up to solve his own problems, and he who would find Christ today must join such efforts.

In distinguishing two trends within the concept of theology in dialogue, we have chosen the "God is dead" school to represent those who advocate transformation of the gospel. This does not mean that all who fit into this trend have abandoned belief in God. Some have transformed Christianity by removing from it belief in the resurrection of Christ or belief that Christ is necessary to salvation. There are two qualifying marks of the transformer. First, he insists that, to be relevant today, theology must not just change how it speaks by finding new ways to present its message, it must change the message itself. Secondly, his criterion for this change is not found in some "purer" form of Christianity such as the Bible or tradition, his criterion is what "modern man" can accept.

As we turn to discuss those whom we have called translators, it must be kept in mind that we are not speaking of a clearly defined school of thought. We are looking at a trend that is beginning to take shape in modern theology. Recent debates have restructured our theological divisions, so that, among those who fit into the translating trend, we find representatives of the new conservatism, of liberalism, and of neo-orthodoxy. There are two characteristics that define the translator. First, he takes as seriously as the transformer the need to enter into dialogue with the modern world and to express Christian faith in terms that speak to modern men. Secondly, he repudiates the claim of the transformer that such dialogue calls for a radical revision in Christian faith. The translator learns from his dialogue with the world *how* he must speak today, but he does not look to the modern world to find *what* he must say. Translators do not agree among themselves on all theological issues, but they agree that their differences cannot be settled by asking what modern man can accept. Modern man cannot be the ultimate authority for what Christians may believe.

Translators are convinced that theology is relevant only when it is able to tell the world something that the world is not already telling itself. As the translators see it, this is a point where the transformers fail. Thus Helmut Gollwitzer, in a review of Robinson's *Honest to God*, says that although Robinson "wishes to make the Christian proclamation worth noticing for men today, he is in danger of making it superfluous instead—and this because he largely reduces it to what a man even without revelation, without considering the phenomenon of Jesus Christ, without listening to the proclamation about him, can say to himself."[17]

Gollwitzer expands this theme in his criticism of certain existentialist theologians. He charges that, in their desire to be relevant, they have transformed the Christian faith. In the Bible, faith is a *new* possibility because it is a dependence upon the Lord who has made himself known. God's act in Christ has opened a new relationship for man. However, Gollwitzer argues, when the attempt is made to pour Christianity into existentialist molds, faith becomes nothing more than an understanding of existence that men can have without Christianity.[18] The translators thus fear that the transformers have not produced a dialogue with the world. Their theology is a monologue in which the modern world speaks to itself.

When the translators make the claim that theology must say something to the world that it is not saying to itself, they raise the question of the truth of Christianity. And here we note a strange tendency among almost all the transformers. They seldom raise the question of truth. As Langdon Gilkey says, they have tended to confuse psychological pressures with logical necessities.[19] No doubt the secular atmosphere of the modern age discourages belief in many aspects of Christianity, but it does not follow from this that the modern world is logically correct.

In recent years a number of books have appeared to argue that, despite changes in the world, the truth of Christian faith can be defended. A new form of apologetics is beginning to appear. The old apologetics hoped that it could begin with evidence that was available to any man, and by an argument that would be obvious to all rational men, it hoped to demonstrate the truth of at least parts of the Christian faith. The classic proofs of God are examples of this form of apologetic. Most of the theologians who accept the contemporary dialogue with the world are convinced that this traditional form of apologetic is no longer effective. We live in an age when the primary differences between men are not in the matter of their conclusions but in the premises from which they begin to reason. We cannot settle our differences by going to the evidence, for what divides us is a question of what constitutes evidence. Thus David Jenkins says that the real problem for belief in God today is a question of epistemology. Many today have a concept of "knowledge" which, by definition, makes knowledge of God impossible.[20]

The new apologetic thus cannot hope to begin simply where man now stands; it must question his very standing place. It must approach him by honestly confessing that it speaks from faith. It must strive to show that the world and life make more sense if we start from Christian premises than if we start from atheistic ones. Typical of such apologetics are the books *The Christian Belief in God*, by Daniel Jenkins, and *The Existence of God as Confessed by Faith*, by Helmut Gollwitzer. Although Jenkins and Gollwitzer differ at several points, they agree that Christian faith must affirm the reality of God's existence and that the Christian can make a persuasive case for belief in God from a standpoint of faith.

The theologians of translation deny the transformers' claim that the change in the world and its thought have made it necessary to abandon the basic affirmations of Christian faith. Daniel Jenkins points out at considerable length that it is false to assume that once, in the times of our forefathers, it was easy to have "simple faith," but that things have changed so that it is now impossible. In fact, all of the objections to Christian faith that are made today were made at its very beginning. For all the changes in man and his thought, there are no new arguments against Christian faith.[21]

The philosopher Paul Holmer develops a similar theme. When transformers would have us abandon belief in God because metaphysical schemes are out of favor today with the intellectuals, Holmer replies that there is no evidence that Christian faith was easier in times of flourishing metaphysical thought. "The depiction of faith in past ages is deceptive: it sustains the illusion that once theology was indubitable, compelling and immediately relevant to all intelligent people, whereas today it is dubious, optional at best, and pertinent only to people who already believe on other than intellectual bases." But, Holmer argues, in all ages Christian faith has called for "courage to believe in a God who redeems, and judges, cares and creates." Christian faith does not depend upon some special technique developed by intellectuals; it is a matter of common sense. "All of us, as a matter of common sense, come to believe in people, the world and perhaps God. We have no special proof for existence, only very ordinary ways to come to the confidences by which we live." Thus it appears to Holmer that the difficulties faced by Christian faith today are quite similar to those always faced and the reasons for believing are as powerful as they ever were.[22]

The question of the degree to which the world has changed also raises the question of who is the "modern man" that is met so frequently in all the discussions of dialogue. The transformers have disagreed among themselves as to who modern man is. Van Buren says, "One wonders where the left-wing existentialist theologians have found their 'modern man.' " In place of the existentialist modern man, van Buren finds the prototype of modern man in the Anglo-Saxon analytical philosopher.

In the light of the failure of the transformers to agree among themselves about modern man, it is not surprising that the translators have pressed this issue. Langdon Gilkey agrees that van Buren has a point against the existentialists, but he goes on to ask where van Buren finds his modern man. Van Buren says that modern man cannot understand language about God, but he remains confident that modern man will find that Jesus and his teachings are relevant to his life. Gilkey objects, "For surely contemporary modern man, committed to the self-orientated values of modern society, would find the self-surrendering, altruistic 'perspective' and 'freedom' of this ancient martyr as strange, as unintelligible, and as offensive as are the old 'myths' in which this story is ordinarily phrased."[23]

Gilkey's comment points to a crucial difference between the translators and the transformers. The transformers seem confident that modern man will accept and live the ideals of Christ when they are freed from "mythical" and "metaphysical" frameworks. As Paul Holmer says, they create the impression "that the whole world would like to become Christian if only the theologians would become modern."[24] But the translators remained convinced that there is a scandal to the Christian faith as it meets us in Christ. Man does not naturally want to be a "man for others," nor does he want to batter down the doors to enter the Kingdom of Heaven. Thus the translators insist that man still needs grace from beyond himself if he is to follow Christ. The Christian ethic cannot live without its theological foundations.

This debate reveals a serious problem for theology that is committed to dialogue. Such theology must ask who is the modern man to which it hopes to speak. But perhaps instead we should speak of modern men rather than of modern man. Never has there been a time when it was more difficult to put one's finger on the essence of the age. There is no world view that is dominant today. This is why theology in our time often reads like the autobiography of the theologian. Those who say that God is dead are describing how they have come to feel about God, and often those who answer them do so by saying that they feel differently. This hardly solves any questions.

Ours is an age of strange contrasts. Twentieth-century man buys the latest model automobile and then places a plastic icon of Jesus on the dashboard to protect him from accidents. A man walks in outer space and returns to describe the good luck charms that he took with him. Theologians say that our age has matured beyond religion, but a drug is discovered that induces religious experiences and a thriving cult grows up to practice religion out of a test tube. Perhaps theology is called to many dialogues with many men. Theologians have been far too hasty in supposing that a Heidegger or a Flew spoke for modern man. Translators thus argue that if we transform the faith so that we make it relevant to one modern group of men, we shall immediately make it irrelevant to most other modern groups.

Another question raised by the translators is whether "modern man," however we define him, is so impressive that we must transform Christian faith to suit him. Is modern man still the old-fashioned sinner dressed up in a space suit? Are the unbelievers of today, like the unbelievers of Paul's days, "blinded by the god of this passing age"? (II Cor. 4:4, NEB)

This point is pressed home by the new conservatives. In an editorial, *Christianity Today* argues that those who would change the Christian message have asked the wrong question and thus come up with the wrong answer. They have asked how they can transform Christianity to enlist modern man and they have come up with the answer, "Restructure the Gospel! rather than *Regenerate the sinner!*"[25] But the conservatives are not alone. Even Erik Routley, who agrees with much of Robinson's *Honest to God*, reminds us that " 'the world' is still a sad and unreconciled world."[26]

Karl Barth likewise challenges us to ask whether it is the Christian gospel or modern man who is irrelevant. Barth suggests that our problem is not with a world come of age but with "a world which *regards* itself as of age (and proves daily that it is precisely not that)."[27] In such a situation, Barth says that it is dangerous to approach modern man "with some sort of gibberish, which, for the moment, is modern," because what we have to say both to other men and to ourselves "is a strange piece of news." The important thing is to see that it is "the *great* piece of news." To translators it appears that the gospels of the transformers have lost all greatness. They are acceptable to modern man precisely because they do not challenge him deeply. Such "radical theology" turns out to be nothing more than a slightly theological expression of what is heard on all sides today.

There is a final critique which the translators might make of the transformers. Most of the transformers have shown a strange reluctance to enter into dialogue with modern believers. Certainly it can be granted that theology must be open to dialogue with the world of unbelief and it must listen to the "cultured despisers" of religion. Nonetheless, we must ask if there is not a serious weakness in the transformers' assumption that all traditional believers are excluded, by definition, from the glorious circle of "modern men." One would have thought that there should be much to learn from those men living in the modern age who have struggled through to an honest and living grasp of the Christian tradition.

An interesting sidelight is thrown on the "God is dead" theology in a statement by Altizer that is quoted with approval by Hamilton. Altizer says that "contemporary theology must be alienated from the Church . . . [and] the theologian must exist outside the Church." Hamilton concludes, "The theologian does not and cannot go to church; he is not interested; he is alienated."[28] Is there a parable here? Does this say that God will seem to be dead to the man who tries to live his life outside of dialogue within the fellowship of those who know and are committed to God through Christ?

Today's theology is committed to the way of dialogue. It has no alternative if it is to be relevant in a fast-changing age. As we look back over the chapters of this book, it is evident that the problems of dialogue are implicit in all the themes that we have discussed. Demythologization and the discussion of history are themes that arise from dialogue with the world. The new conservatives are seeking dialogue with their world and a way to translate without transforming the gospel. The revival of the doctrine of sanctification seeks to speak to the world through actions as well as through words. Worldly or secularized Christianity is by its very nature involved in dialogue with the world in which it finds itself.

It is too early to forecast what the results of the contemporary dialogue will be. Already it is apparent that theologians who are most concerned about dialogue are more prone to speak than to listen. Having heard a little from someone that appeals to them, they crown him as "Mr. Modern Man" and then speak only to him. Perhaps theology has for too long been the monopoly of seminaries and, to a lesser degree, of college departments of religion. The dialogue needs to be extended so that it involves laymen, believing and unbelieving. We also need more contributions from the parish clergymen. Too often they have been intimidated into thinking that they can make no theological contributions, but they are often more likely to know what modern men are really thinking than are their brothers in the academic world.

In a serious theological dialogue many things may happen. It could be that the church will be revealed to be irrelevant and outdated. It could be that modern man will be exposed as irrelevant and in desperate need of salvation. More likely it will appear that there is fault upon both the side of the church and of the unbeliever today. At this point we can expect that the church will try to gloss over its own shortcomings by blaming its failures on the hardness of men's hearts. Where that happens we need the persistent voices of the transformers. They will always appear strange and annoying in the life of the church, but they can serve as a needed goad to spur the church toward continuing reformation. At the same time, the dialogue will tempt many to cast their lot with the god of this passing age. Where that happens, we need the persistent voices of those who, while ready to translate the faith for the modern times, are not prepared "to practice cunning or to tamper with God's word" (II Cor. 4:2).

Notes

Notes

Chapter I. Theology in Transit

1. See Edgar S. Brightman, *A Philosophy of Religion* (Prentice-Hall, Inc., 1940), pp. 22–26.

Chapter II. The Demythologization Debate

1. See Hans Werner Bartsch, ed., *Kerygma and Myth: A Theological Debate;* with contributions by Rudolf Bultmann *et al.,* tr. by Reginald H. Fuller (London: S.P.C.K., 1953), Vol. I, pp. 1–44.

2. See Hans Werner Bartsch, ed., *Kerygma and Myth: A Theological Debate;* with contributions by Rudolf Bultmann *et al.,* tr. by Reginald H. Fuller (London: S.P.C.K., 1962), Vol. II, pp. 83–84.

3. Bartsch, *Kerygma and Myth,* Vol. II, pp. 6–7.

4. Karl Jaspers and Rudolf Bultmann, *Myth and Christianity: An Inquiry Into the Possibility of Religion Without Myth* (The Noonday Press, 1958), p. 60.

5. Bartsch, *Kerygma and Myth,* Vol. I, p. 10, note 2.

6. *Ibid.,* p. 197.

7. For the most ambitious attempt to demonstrate that Bultmann does use the concept of myth consistently, see Schubert Ogden, *Christ Without Myth* (Harper & Brothers, 1961), pp. 28 ff. For a summary of some reasons for denying Bultmann's consistency, see John Macquarrie, *The Scope of Demythologizing* (Harper & Brothers, 1960), pp. 200 ff.

8. Bartsch, *Kerygma and Myth,* Vol. I, p. 211.

9. See Friedrich Gogarten, *Demythologizing and History,* tr. by Neville Horton Smith (Charles Scribner's Sons, 1955), Ch. VIII.

10. Helmut Gollwitzer, *The Existence of God as Confessed by Faith*, tr. by James W. Leitch (The Westminster Press, 1965), pp. 48–49.

11. *Ibid.*, p. 95.

12. Bartsch, *Kerygma and Myth*, Vol. II, p. 28.

13. See Carl E. Braaten and Roy A. Harrisville, eds. and trs., *Kerygma and History* (Abingdon Press, 1962), p. 72.

14. Jaspers and Bultmann, *op. cit.*, p. 81.

15. Martin Luther, in Theodore Tappert, ed. and tr., *The Book of Concord* (Muhlenberg Press, 1959), p. 440.

16. *Ibid.*, p. 441.

17. Karl Barth, *Church Dogmatics*, Vol. III, Part 2, p. 443. Barth's *Dogmatics* in the English version is edited by G. W. Bromiley and T. F. Torrance and is published by T. & T. Clark, Edinburgh, and by Charles Scribner's Sons. All future references are to the English translation and give only the volumes and part numbers and page references.

18. Bartsch, *Kerygma and Myth*, Vol. I, pp. 38–39.

19. *Ibid.*, p. 41. Emphasis is Bultmann's.

20. *Ibid.*, p. 42.

21. *Ibid.*, p. 112.

22. *Ibid.*, p. 196.

23. *Ibid.*, p. 40.

24. *Ibid.*, p. 200.

25. Rudolf Bultmann, *Essays: Philosophical and Theological*, tr. by J. C. G. Grieg (The Macmillan Company, 1955), p. 241. Emphasis is Bultmann's.

26. *Ibid.*, p. 257.

27. Bartsch, *Kerygma and Myth*, Vol. II, p. 259.

28. Bultmann, *Essays*, p. 258.

29. Bartsch, *Kerygma and Myth*, Vol. I, p. 192.

30. Jaspers and Bultmann, *op. cit.*, p. 9.

31. *Ibid.*, pp. 8–9.

32. See James M. Robinson and John B. Cobb, Jr., eds., *New Frontiers in Theology: Discussions Among German and American Theologians*, Vol. I: *The Later Heidegger and Theology* (Harper & Row, Publishers, Inc., 1963), especially Chs. 1 and 2.

33. Bartsch, *Kerygma and Myth*, Vol. I, p. 25.

34. Ogden, *op. cit.*, p. 146.

35. *Ibid.*, p. 138.

36. Bartsch, *Kerygma and Myth*, Vol. I, pp. 24–25.

37. *Ibid.*, p. 150.

38. Martin Heidegger, *Being and Time,* tr. by John Macquarrie and E. Robinson (Harper & Brothers, 1962), pp. 325–348.

39. *Ibid.,* pp. 317–325.

40. Gollwitzer, *op. cit.,* p. 33.

41. Bartsch, *Kerygma and Myth,* Vol. I, p. 214.

42. P. M. van Buren, *The Secular Meaning of the Gospel* (The Macmillan Company, 1963), p. 68.

43. Harvey Cox, *The Secular City* (The Macmillan Company, 1965), pp. 248–257.

44. For example, see James M. Robinson and John B. Cobb, Jr., eds., *New Frontiers in Theology: Discussions Among German and American Theologians* (Vol. II, The New Hermeneutic) (Harper & Row, Publishers, Inc., 1964).

CHAPTER III. HISTORY AND KERYGMA

1. See Carl E. Braaten, *History and Hermeneutics* (Vol. II, New Directions in Theology Today) (The Westminster Press, 1966).

2. Bartsch, *Kerygma and Myth,* Vol. I, p. 22. Emphasis is Bultmann's.

3. Joachim Jeremias, *The Problem of the Historical Jesus,* tr. by Norman Perrin (Fortress Press, 1964), p. 1.

4. Albert Schweitzer, *The Quest of the Historical Jesus,* tr. by W. Montgomery (The Macmillan Company, 1948), p. 4.

5. Gerhard Ebeling, *The Nature of Faith,* tr. by R. G. Smith (Muhlenberg Press, 1961), p. 46.

6. See Rudolf Bultmann, "The Primitive Christian Kerygma and the Historical Jesus," in C. E. Braaten and R. A. Harrisville, eds. and trs., *The Historical Jesus and the Kerygmatic Christ* (Abingdon Press, 1964), pp. 15–42.

7. *Ibid.,* p. 18.

8. This point is well documented by Hugh Anderson, *Jesus and Christian Origins* (Oxford University Press, 1964), Ch. 4, especially pp. 180–181.

9. Ethelbert Stauffer, *Jesus and His Story,* tr. by R. and C. Winston (Alfred A. Knopf, Inc., 1959), pp. 174–195.

10. Heinz Zahrnt, *The Historical Jesus,* tr. by J. S. Bowden (Harper & Row, Publishers, Inc., 1963), p. 138.

11. Braaten and Harrisville, *The Historical Jesus and the Kerygmatic Christ,* p. 7.

12. Zahrnt, *op. cit.,* p. 99.

13. S. Laeuchli, "Unsolved Contradictions," a review of Ebeling's *Ein Gespräch mit Rudolf Bultmann, Interpretation,* Vol. XVII, No. 5 (July 1963), p. 326.

14. Zahrnt, *op. cit.,* p. 87.

15. Markus Barth and Verne H. Fletcher, *Acquittal by Resurrection* (Holt, Rinehart and Winston, Inc., 1963), pp. 152–153.

16. John Knox, *The Church and the Reality of Christ* (Harper & Brothers, 1962), pp. 22 ff.

17. Plutarch, *The Lives of the Noble Grecians and Romans,* tr. by John Dryden (Modern Library, Inc., n.d.), p. 3.

18. Gerhard Ebeling, *Word and Faith,* tr. by W. Leitch (Fortress Press, 1963), p. 291 (footnote).

19. Richard Reinhold Niebuhr, *Resurrection and Historical Reason: A Study of Theological Method* (Charles Scribner's Sons, 1957), pp. 13–14.

20. Zahrnt, *op. cit.,* p. 121.

CHAPTER IV. THE NEW FACE OF CONSERVATISM

1. John B. Cobb, Jr., *Living Options in Protestant Theology: A Survey of Methods* (The Westminster Press, 1962), p. 13.

2. A. Berkeley Mickelsen, *Interpreting the Bible* (Wm. B. Eerdmans Publishing Company, 1963), p. 349.

3. See Herman Dooyeweerd, *A New Critique of Theoretical Thought,* tr. by David H. Freeman, and others, 4 vols. (Presbyterian & Reformed Publishing Co., 1953).

4. See R. B. Case, "Neo-Evangelicalism: New Life on the Right," *Christian Advocate,* April 26, 1962, pp. 7–8.

5. E. J. Carnell, *An Introduction to Christian Apologetics* (Wm. B. Eerdmans Publishing Company, 1948), pp. 193–194.

6. E. J. Carnell, *The Case for Orthodox Theology* (The Westminster Press, 1959), pp. 97–98.

7. Mickelsen, *op. cit.,* p. 45.

8. See Carl Henry, ed., *Basic Christian Doctrines* (Holt, Rinehart and Winston, Inc., 1962), p. 253.

9. Carnell, *The Case for Orthodox Theology,* pp. 52–64.

10. See, for example, P. E. Hughes, "The Knowledge of God: The Inspiration of the Bible," in Henry, *op. cit.,* pp. 14–20.

11. Dewey M. Beegle, *The Inspiration of Scripture* (The Westminster Press, 1963), p. 167.

12. *Ibid.,* p. 158.

13. See *Christianity Today*, Vol. VII, No. 15 (April 26, 1963).

14. *Ibid.*, p. 47.

15. J. Baillie, *The Idea of Revelation in Recent Thought* (Columbia University Press, 1956), p. 92.

16. See K. Kantzer, "The Authority of the Bible" in M. C. Tenney, ed., *The Word for This Century* (Oxford University Press, 1960), p. 34.

17. *Ibid.*, p. 38.

18. Mickelsen, *op. cit.*, p. 70.

19. *Ibid.*, p. 8.

20. *Ibid.*, p. 67.

21. R. H. King, *The Omission of the Holy Spirit from Reinhold Niebuhr's Theology* (Philosophical Library, Inc., 1964), p. 9.

22. See C. Henry, "Chaos in European Theology: The Deterioration of Barth's Defenses," *Christianity Today*, Vol. IX, No. 1 (Oct. 9, 1964), pp. 15–19.

23. J. G. Machen, "History and Faith," *Christianity Today*, Vol. VIII, No. 24 (Sept. 11, 1964), p. 23.

24. *Ibid.*, p. 26.

25. *Ibid.*, p. 27.

CHAPTER V. SANCTIFICATION REDISCOVERED

1. See Pierre Berton, *The Comfortable Pew* (Toronto: McClelland and Stewart, 1965), especially Chs. 1 and 2.

2. Barth, *Church Dogmatics*, Vol. IV, Part 2, p. 505.

3. See Dietrich Bonhoeffer, *The Cost of Discipleship*, tr. by R. H. Fuller (London: SCM Press, Ltd., 1959), especially pp. 35–47.

4. Barth, *Church Dogmatics*, Vol. IV, Part 2, p. 516.

5. L. Harold DeWolf, *The Case for Theology in Liberal Perspective* (The Westminster Press, 1959), p. 130.

6. Barth, *Church Dogmatics*, Vol. IV, Part 2, p. 508.

7. Langdon Gilkey, *How the Church Can Minister to the World Without Losing Itself* (Harper & Row, Publishers, Inc., 1964), p. 47.

8. Bonhoeffer, *The Cost of Discipleship*, p. 40.

9. Barth, *Church Dogmatics*, Vol. IV, Part 2, 549.

10. *Ibid.*, p. 550.

11. For example see Henry Steele Commager, "A Historian Looks at Our Political Morality," *Saturday Review*, July 10, 1965, pp. 16–18.

12. Charles C. West, *Communism and the Theologians* (The Westminster Press, 1958), pp. 168–171, 240–242.

13. Barth, *Church Dogmatics,* Vol. IV, Part 2, p. 813.

14. See J. H. Burtness and J. P. Kildahl, eds., *The New Community in Christ* (Augsburg Publishing House, 1963), p. 89.

15. Emil Brunner, *The Christian Doctrine of the Church, Faith, and the Consummation (Church Dogmatics,* Vol. III), tr. by David Cairns and T. H. L. Parker (The Westminster Press, 1962), p. 9.

16. *Ibid.,* p. 296.

17. *Ibid.,* p. 21.

CHAPTER VI.
BEYOND RELIGION TO WORLDLY CHRISTIANITY

1. Dean Peerman, "Church and World," *The Christian Century,* Vol. LXXXI, No. 4 (Jan. 22, 1964), pp. 104–105.

2. See Alan Richardson, *An Introduction to the Theology of the New Testament* (Harper & Brothers, 1958), pp. 207–208, 211–214.

3. Barth, *Church Dogmatics,* Vol. I, Part 2, pp. 280–361.

4. *Ibid.,* p. 330.

5. *Ibid.,* p. 321.

6. *Ibid.,* p. 326.

7. Barth, *Church Dogmatics,* Vol. III, Part 2, p. 410.

8. Barth, *Church Dogmatics,* Vol. III, Part 3, pp. 255–256.

9. Dietrich Bonhoeffer, *Prisoner for God,* ed. by Eberhard Bethge, tr. by Reginald H. Fuller (The Macmillan Company, 1953), pp. 146–147.

10. *Ibid.,* p. 162.

11. *Ibid.,* p. 146.

12. *Ibid.,* p. 167.

13. Barth, *Church Dogmatics,* Vol. I, Part 2, p. 321.

14. Bonhoeffer, *Prisoner for God,* p. 123.

15. *Ibid.,* p. 140.

16. Daniel Jenkins, *Beyond Religion* (The Westminster Press, 1962), p. 19.

17. Cox, *The Secular City,* p. 167.

18. *Ibid.,* pp. 125–126.

19. Berton, *op. cit.,* p. 51.

20. C. Williams, *Where in the World* (Office of Publication and Distribution, National Council of the Churches of Christ in the U.S.A., 1963), p. 12.

21. S. H. Miller, *The Dilemma of Modern Belief* (Harper & Row, Publishers, Inc., 1963), p. 46.

22. William Hamilton, "The Death of God Theology," in *The Christian Scholar*, Vol. XLVIII, No. 1 (Spring, 1965), p. 40.

23. Jenkins, *op. cit.*, p. 10.

24. Cox, *op. cit.*, pp. 20–21.

25. L. Gilkey, *How the Church Can Minister to the World Without Losing Itself*, p. 2.

26. Williams, *op. cit.*, pp. 28–29.

CHAPTER VII. THEOLOGY IN DIALOGUE

1. Berton, *op. cit.*, p. 117.

2. Paul Tillich, *Systematic Theology* (The University of Chicago Press, 1951), Vol. I, pp. 59–66.

3. John A. T. Robinson, *Honest to God* (The Westminster Press, 1963), pp. 7–8.

4. *Ibid.*, p. 50.

5. *Ibid.*, Ch. 6.

6. *Ibid.*, pp. 92 ff.

7. John A. T. Robinson, *The New Reformation?* (The Westminster Press, 1965), p. 50.

8. *Ibid.*, p. 115.

9. Thomas J. J. Altizer, "Creative Negation in Theology," *The Christian Century*, Vol. LXXXII, No. 27 (July 7, 1965), p. 865.

10. William Hamilton, *loc. cit.*, p. 45.

11. Van Buren, *op. cit.*, p. 84.

12. Hamilton, *loc. cit.*, p. 46.

13. Van Buren, *op. cit.*, p. 198.

14. Altizer, *op. cit.*, p. 866.

15. Van Buren, *op. cit.*, pp. 193–200.

16. Hamilton, *loc. cit.*, p. 38.

17. Gollwitzer, *op. cit.*, p. 251.

18. *Ibid.*, pp. 62–64.

19. L. Gilkey, *How the Church Can Minister to the World Without Losing Itself*, p. 54 (footnote).

20. David Jenkins, "Whither the Doctrine of God Now?" in *New Theology*, ed. by M. E. Marty and D. G. Peerman (The Macmillan Company, 1965), pp. 65 ff. See also, David Jenkins, *A Guide to the Debate About God* (The Westminster Press, 1966).

21. Daniel Jenkins, *The Christian Belief in God* (The Westminster Press, 1963), pp. 128 ff.

22. See P. L. Holmer, "Contra the New Theologies," *The Christian Century*, Vol. LXXXII, No. 11 (March 17, 1965), p. 330.

23. L. Gilkey, "A New Linguistic Madness," in Marty and Peerman, *New Theology*, No. 2, p. 44.

24. Holmer, *loc. cit.*, p. 331.

25. *Christianity Today*, Vol. IX, No. 21 (July 16, 1965), p. 1075.

26. E. Routley, *The Man for Others* (Oxford University Press, 1964), p. 87.

27. Karl Barth, *The Humanity of God* (John Knox Press, 1960), pp. 58–59.

28. William Hamilton, "Tomorrow's Theologian, Thursday's Child," in *Theology Today*, Vol. XX, No. 4 (Jan. 1964), p. 490.

Index

Index